D0469631

Biplanes (pp. 2–15)

Agricultural Planes (pp. 14–21)

Low-Wing Singles (pp. 22–51)

FIXED GEAR

Tail-Draggers (pp. 22–25)

Tricycle (pp. 24–33, 38–39)

RETRACTABLE

Tail-Draggers (pp. 42–51)

Tricycle (pp. 28–47)

High-Wing Singles (pp. 52–83)

FIXED GEAR

Tail-Draggers (pp. 52–73)

Tricycle (pp. 76–81)

RETRACTABLE

Tricycle (pp. 78–83)

Amphibians (pp. 84–91)

Twins (pp. 92–139)

SMALL

Low-Wing (pp. 92–113)

High-Wing (pp. 112–115)

Continued on back endpapers

A Field Guide
to Airplanes
of North America

A Field Guide to

Airplanes

of North America

SECOND EDITION

M. R. Montgomery
and Gerald L. Foster

Illustrated by Gerald L. Foster

HOUGHTON MIFFLIN COMPANY

Boston   New York

For information about permission to reproduce selections from this
book, write to Permissions, Houghton Mifflin Company, 215 Park Ave-
nue South, New York, New York 10003.

Library of Congress Cataloging-in-Publication Data

Montgomery, M. R.
    A field guide to airplanes of North America / M. R. Montgomery
and Gerald L. Foster ; illustrated by Gerald L. Foster. — 2nd ed., rev.
and updated.
        p.   cm.
    Includes bibliographical references and index.
    ISBN 0-395-62889-X (cloth). — ISBN 0-395-62888-1 (pbk.)
    1. Airplanes—Recognition.   2. Helicopters—Recognition.
I. Foster, Gerald L.   II. Title.
TL671.M64   1992
629.133'34—dc20   92-4934
                                CIP

Printed in the United States of America

HOR 10 9 8 7 6 5 4 3 2

Contents

Introduction

The purpose of this revised and expanded field guide is simple: to encourage persons of any age to *identify* all of the factory-built aircraft they are likely to see anywhere in North America — small general-aviation planes, airliners, business jets, and military aircraft. For this second edition, we have included civilian and military helicopters, a complex but interesting order of aircraft.

While this is not the only aircraft identification guide in the history of publishing, it is unique. Like the Peterson Field Guides, it is devoted to a single geographical area. Although many of the aircraft in this book are seen throughout the world, we have excluded foreign aircraft that are never, or very rarely, seen in North American airspace. Guides to "all the world's" aircraft eliminate all of the older and rarer planes, they lump complex series into an indistinct and blurred composite aircraft, and they confuse readers by showing them Russian or European planes that simply do not operate in our skies. Just as bird guides do not include the fauna in zoological parks, this guide does not include museum pieces. It is a book about what's up there now, and we know it is also useful worldwide, particularly for older aircraft built during the era when the United States dominated the industry.

We have used two simple principles in choosing aircraft for inclusion: We depict all aircraft of which thirty or more examples still fly in United States, Mexico, and Canada; and, because interest is heightened when one actually flies in a plane, we have included every commercial airliner for which you may someday buy a ticket.

One single class of fixed-wing aircraft is not fully covered, the "home-builts." Their variety is too great, and builders may modify them to suit their own tastes. However, several of the planes included here have been both factory- and home-built, and that is noted in the text. In particular, we have covered the most popular home-built biplanes, because they are patterned after production aircraft of the 1930s and 1940s.

How to Use This Book

Aircraft are grouped by both their use and their appearance. The book begins with the small airplanes in what is usually called "general aviation," starting with biplanes and followed by agricultural planes (including agricultural biplanes). Single-engine propeller-driven planes are grouped by such quickly visible field marks as whether they have wings mounted on top of the fuselage or at the bottom; by landing gear, fixed or retractable; by type of gear, tail-dragging or tricycle. Several manufacturers have made essentially the same plane with fixed or retractable gear, and these are grouped in the transitional pages between types of aircraft.

Both the multiengine props and jets are grouped by size. While there is a certain charm to keeping all twin, fuselage-mounted, swept-wing jets together, that would have put aircraft as large as a stretched MD80 carrying nearly two hundred passengers next to the much smaller, not really similar, Falcon 20 business jet that seats eight.

Special-purpose military aircraft — combat, transportation, observation — are grouped together. However, dozens of commercial and general-aviation aircraft, planes and helicopters, are acquired by the military for transportation, often of VIPs. Pure military planes and helicopters just don't look like jetliners or business jets. Something conventional-looking, but wearing military insignia or camouflage, can be easily identified by looking for it in the appropriate civilian section of the book.

We have avoided technical language whenever possible, and would just as soon think of "vertical stabilizers" as tail fins, and call them that. However, some useful field marks have their own aeronautical terms: we should define "chord," "dihedral," "fairing," and "nacelle."

The best way to describe a wing that is the same width along its entire length is to refer to its "constant chord" (from the geometrical term describing the distance across the bottom of a curve, measured in a straight line; all wings are curved across the top).

Another useful technical term is "dihedral," which describes wings or tail planes ("horizontal stabilizers") that angle upward, so that the wing tip is elevated above the root of the wing at the fuselage. Even very slight dihedrals in small tail planes, as well as in long wings, are quite noticeable from a distance.

The word "fairing" appears often, and is an old word from ship's architecture adapted to aeronautics. A fairing is simply a smoothed-out or streamlined connection between two parts of a vessel — ship or aircraft — that often conceals structural bracing. Fairings are common at wing roots and where engines are inserted into wings. The engine housings are called "nacelles" (from an old French word meaning "little boat," which captures the tapering shape rather nicely).

Identifying a particular aircraft usually requires recognizing a combination of two or more field marks. For some similar models, you may be reduced to counting passenger windows or noting the shape of the windows. The easiest place to identify planes is at an airport, just as the easiest place to identify birds is at a near-at-hand bird feeder. And, as happens with birding, once you have made a positive identification of a perching bird and then have seen it fly, some of the little field marks become irrelevant, and you recognize the bird as a whole, not just as the sum of its field-mark parts. British birders, for reasons unclear, refer to this as the "jizz" of the bird. We like to think of it as the (hard g) gestalt, a German word for the unique presence of a person or a thing. A stretched DC8, once you have seen one nearby and then watched it disappear into the distance, will always be instantly identifiable at any range — a long skinny fuselage balanced on relatively small wings.

There is no rigid order for using the field marks. We suggest that you thumb through the sections of the book, get a sense of where the high-wings and low-wings, propellers and jets, fixed and retractable airplanes are located, and browse the field marks for a variety of aircraft *before* you start to use the book. Get a sense of the useful field marks, and try to find them all at once — this will work much better than some rigid litany of "wing, tail, landing gear, window . . ." As with any field guide, familiarity with the book is the best system.

A Field Guide
to Airplanes
of North America

Beech 17 Staggerwing
(Navy GB-1, Air Force C-43)

Length: 26'9" (8.13 m)   *Wingspan:* 32' (9.76 m)   *Cruising speed:* 201 mph (323 km/h)

Rare. Large; *reversed staggerwing (lower wing forward of upper); enclosed cabin; solid wing struts.*

The Rolls-Royce of biplanes. Performance data is for the most powerful versions with 450-horsepower engines. First flown in 1932 with fixed landing gear; never seen today without the electrically operated retractable gear. Various models have slight dimensional changes, but all are clearly Staggerwings. Once a popular float and ski plane. A few postwar models, last produced in 1948, have leather upholstery and other comforts.

Note: Any cabin biplane that is not a Beech 17 (reversed staggerwing) is a Waco.

Any cabin biplane with an upper wing much longer and deeper than the bottom wing is a late-model Waco C (custom) biplane.

All other cabin biplanes, with wings of equal width and normal stagger are Waco S (standard) or very early C (custom) planes.

Waco Late C Series

Length: 27'7" (8.42 m)   *Wingspan:* upper, 34'9" (10.57 m); lower, 24'6" (7.47 m)   *Cruising speed:* 155 mph (249 km/h)

Rare. A *cabin biplane* with a *noticeably shorter and narrower lower wing* (compare with Waco S series, below); *fixed landing gear; N wing struts,* plus a *heavy brace* from the base of the N strut to the upper wing.

One of four basic types of Waco biplanes, the late C (custom cabin) series is the only one with the very small, normally staggered lower wing. Built throughout the 1930s. The fixed gear is usually seen with streamlined wheel pants. Proper restoration includes the straight-line striping from the engine cowling to the tail plane. A few were in U.S. and foreign military service, but for the famous WWII basic trainer, see the Waco UPF7, next page.

Waco S Series, Early C Series

Length: 25'3" (7.71 m)   *Wingspan:* upper, 33'3" (10.15 m); lower, 28'3" (8.62 m)   *Cruising speed:* 133 mph (214 km/h)

Rare. *Cabin biplane* with *slightly shorter lower wing;* wings of *equal width (chord); N struts, plus solid brace.*

The S (standard) and early C (custom) Waco biplanes are handsome, symmetrical, and remarkable for their lack of unusual features. They have very similar upper and lower wings, typical struts, and a conventional cabin. Usually restored with the Waco signature stripe from cowling to tail. Both wings have a matching, very slight dihedral. Although they were not supplied with streamlined wheel pants, like the C series, you may see one that's been modified. Concentrate on the wings.

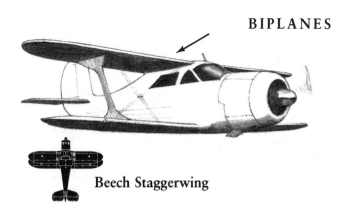

Beech Staggerwing

Waco Late C Series

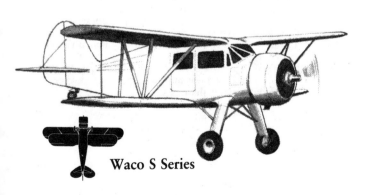

Waco S Series

Boeing/Stearman Kaydet
(military PT-13, PT-17, PT-18)

Length: 24'10" (7.58 m)   *Wingspan:* upper, 32'2" (9.82 m); lower, 1' shorter overall   *Cruising speed:* 103 mph (166km/h)

Fairly common. The *normally staggered wings of almost equal length,* combined with the *unbraced heavy landing gear* and the *N struts without an aileron connector,* separate the Kaydet from the somewhat similar biplanes of the 1930s and 1940s. Compare the three aircraft that follow below.

More than 10,000 Stearmans were built from the early 1930s through WWII; model designators indicate engines of different horsepower. A jointly procured trainer for the Navy and the Army Air Corps, many are seen restored to their WWII paint scheme — Air Force blue fuselage and Navy yellow wings with service markings. Note that although the cockpits are large and deep, there is no turtleback behind the rear cockpit.

Naval Aircraft Factory N3N1, N3N3

Length: 25'11" (7.96 m)   *Wingspan:* 34' (10.38 m)   *Cruising speed:* 92 mph (148 km/h)

Rare. *Normally staggered wings identical in length and width (chord); N struts* with *aileron connector; skinny braced landing gear without wheel pants; no engine cowling.*

Once used extensively as agricultural aircraft, the government-built N3Ns are collector's items. A proper restoration is all yellow with Navy insignia. The last biplane in U.S. service, until 1958, as a float plane at the U.S. Naval Academy, Annapolis. All midshipmen had to spend ten hours flying in the "Yellow Peril" whether they were aviators or not — for many, an experience that was equaled only by submarine escape training for sheer terror.

Waco UPF7, YPF7 (military trainer PT-14), Model D

Length: 23'1" (7.06 m)   *Wingspan:* 30' (9.14 m); lower, 26'10" (8.18 m)   *Cruising speed:* 123 mph (198 km/h)

Fairly common. *Lower wing noticeably shorter;* look for the *large rectangular cutout in the upper wing;* designed for easier access to the forward cockpit; *longer nosed* than the early F series; may or may not have engine cowling.

Although a military trainer in WWII, not as common as the Stearman Kaydets or the Naval Factory N3N series. Very popular primary trainer with the WWII government Civilian Pilot Training Program. A sports type (Waco model D) was built with streamlined wheel pants and lighter construction materials.

Boeing/Stearman Kaydet

Naval Aircraft
Factory N3N3

Waco UPF7, PT-14

Classic Waco F-5

Length: 23'4" (7.10 m)   *Wingspan:* upper, 30' (9.14 m); lower, 26'10" (8.18 m)   *Cruising speed:* 110 mph (198 km/h)

Least common, but newest, of the F series. *Lower wing slightly shorter than upper, engine cowling shows bumps, never smooth, always with streamlined wheel pants;* up close, can be distinguished from the old F series by the *added navigation lights.*

Built under the original Model F-5 certification, but with modern corrosion-proof metals, hydraulic brakes, self-starting engine, fireproofing forward of the engine wall. Classic Aircraft, of Lansing, Michigan, recreated the Waco, and have more than 30 on airfields from Hawaii to Maine. Rarest in the Pacific Northwest (where open cockpits are wet cockpits).

Waco Early F Series

Length: 20'9" (6.31 m)   *Wingspan:* 29'6" (9 m)   *Cruising speed:* 90 mph (145 km/h)

Rare. May be confused with the Waco UPF7 or the naval aircraft trainer, *but very stubby nosed; wings of equal length; N brace with aileron connector; small circular cutout in top wing* for access to front cockpit; distinct turtleback behind rear cockpit.

A popular sportster and trainer from early 1930s, the early F series is popular with restorers, but much less common than the Waco UPF7 military trainers, which it slightly resembles. Built with and without engine cowlings, some with ring cowlings, some with streamlined cowling, but typically with exposed radial engine cylinder heads. Landing gear usually bare.

Travel Air 4000

Length: 24'2" (7.35 m)   *Wingspan:* 34'8" (10.53 m)   *Cruising speed:* 100 mph (161 km/h)

Rare. *Looks distinctly antique;* almost always shows the *elephant-ear upper wing tip and tail fin; N bracing,* plus aileron control transfer bar; some built with conventional speed wings, but these show the elephant-ear tail; a few with conventionally rounded tails, but these always show the upper wing elephant ear, which is an extension of the aileron; both wings straight, lower wing noticeably shorter and slightly narrower.

The Travel Air was built in a variety of versions, including passenger carriers, with a two-man forward cockpit. All originals and accurate restorations have either radial (in the more numerous 4000 series) or in-line (in the very rare 2000 series) water-cooled engines. A small radiator extends below the fuselage, just forward of the cockpit area. The high, quickly rising turtleback is unique.

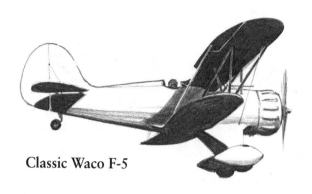

Classic Waco F-5

Waco Early F Series QCF2

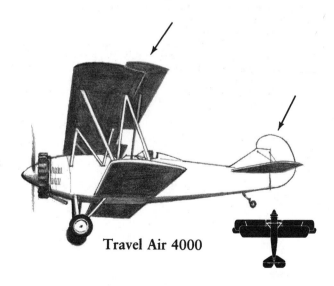

Travel Air 4000

Fleet Finch Trainer

Length: 21'8" (7.1 m)   *Wingspan:* both, 28' (8.53 m)   *Cruising speed:* 98 mph (158 km/h)

Rare. *Very stubby nosed; straight wings of equal length; lower wing with noticeable dihedral; N bracing; no aileron control* transfer bar. Early models, built in the U.S., have elephant-ear tails.

Made in the U.S. in the early 1930s, then in Canada, where more than 600 were built from 1938 to 1941 for RCAF flight training. Many restored Canadian-built WWII trainers have a single sliding canopy that covers both cockpits; other models have simple, flat-glass, three-sided windshields. Once a popular ski and float plane.

Meyers OTW

Length: 22'8" (6.91 m)   *Wingspan:* both, 30' (9.14 m)   *Cruising speed:* 100 mph (161 km/h)

Rare. Combines *all-aluminum fuselage* with *fabric wings;* wings are identical, with slight dihedral; *the landing gear strut shock-absorbing piston,* which extends up to the forward cockpit, *is diagnostic.*

Only 102 "Out to Wins" were built during WWII, all for the Civilian Pilot Training Program, and half of them are still registered — some flying, the others being restored. Their use as crop dusters after WWII contributed to the loss of many of the aircraft. Manufactured in Romulus, Michigan, from 1940 to 1944 by people who had never before, and never afterward, built airplanes.

de Havilland DH82 Tiger Moth, PT-24

Length: 23'11" (7.29 m)   *Wingspan:* 29'4" (8.94 m)   *Cruising speed:* 90 mph (145 km/h)

Fairly common for an antique biplane. *Swept wings of equal length; stout double-bar wing connectors (not N);* the entire plane gives a distinct impression of slimness, including the in-line engine and the fancifully tapered tail fin and tail planes.

The Tiger Moth, a 130-horsepower version of the 1920s Gipsy Moth, first flew in 1932 and was produced through WWII, totaling more than 8000 planes. The standard RAF and Royal Navy primary trainer; a few hundred in USAAF, designated PT-24. Surplus Moths were the backbone of private aviation in Great Britain and Canada after WWII. The bulky apparatus over the cockpit that connects the left and right wings is the fuel tank.

Fleet Finch
Trainer

Meyers OTW

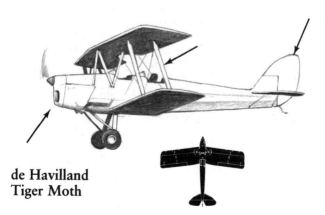

de Havilland
Tiger Moth

Great Lakes Sport Trainer, Baby Lakes

Great Lakes specifications: *Length:* 20'4" (6.2 m)   *Wingspan:* 26'8"
(8.13 m)   *Cruising speed:* 110 mph (177 km/h).   Baby Lakes
specifications: *Length:* 13'9" (4.10 m)   *Wingspan:* 16'8" (5.08)
Cruising speeds: various, depending on optional engines

The original Great Lakes, built between 1929 and 1932, and the
revival, built between 1974 and 1978, were tandem dual controls;
the Baby Lakes is ⁶/₁₀ their size and is either single or dual. They
share the identifying combination: *top wing swept, over straight bottom wing and N struts.* Owners can modify struts to a single one,
thereby possibly causing confusion with the Pitts Special (next entry).
Call it a Pitts/Lake, especially if the wheel struts on the Great Lakes
have been covered with streamlining sheet metal. Original Great
Lakes had ailerons on the lower wing only; some have been modified
and show the aileron transfer control bar next to the N brace.

Although only 200 of the original Great Lakes trainers were built,
they dominated acrobatics and closed-course racing in the U.S. in the
1930s. The company was revived and several versions, of greatly
varying horsepower, were built. You may even see a one-seat, full-size
Great Lakes. Concentrate on the wing and wing strut combination.
It's unique.

Aviat Pitts S-1, S-2 Special

S-1 specifications: *Length:* 15'5" (4.7 m)   *Wingspan:* 17'4" (5.28 m)
Cruising speed: 140 mph (225 km/h)

Usually seen in the S-1 (single-seat) version. A chunky little plane.
The unique combination is *top wing swept and slightly longer than
straight lower wing; single wing strut plus aileron control transfer
bar. Optional fuselage/upper wing bracing may originate from two
points on the wing rather than the typical N bracing.* The turtleback
is high and distinctive.

The single-seat S-1 is unique in that it is available as a factory-built
and certified plane or as plans or kits for the home builder. The S-2
dual control is only available through the factory. They have been
flown with all manner of engines, up to 450 horsepower; became the
premier aerobatic airplane in the 1960s. Home-built Pitts Specials
may show additional bracing and wiring, probably out of a deep
sense of insecurity on the part of the builder.

Aviat Christen Eagle I, II

Eagle II (two-seater), specifications: *Length:* 18'6" (5.64 m)
Wingspan: 19'11" (6.07 m)   *Cruising speed:* 158 mph (254 km/h)

A kit-builder's plane. The one-seat Eagle I, introduced in late 1982,
has *both wings swept, single strut, and bubble canopy.* It's almost always seen with Eagle paint job, *long-nosed, large propeller spinner.*

BIPLANES

**Great Lakes
Sport Trainer**

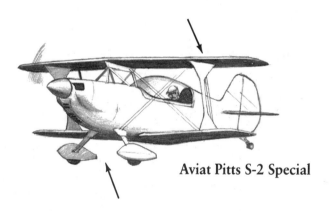

Baby Lakes

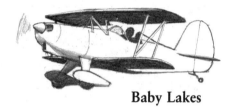

Aviat Pitts S-2 Special

Aviat Christen Eagle II

Stolp Starduster, Acroduster

Starduster 100 specifications: *Length:* 16'6" (5.03 m)   *Wingspan:* upper, 19' (5.79 m); lower, 18' (5.49 m)   *Cruising speed:* 132 mph (212 km/h)

A family of home-builts. The Startdusters and the more strongly constructed aerobatic Acrodusters have *unequal span wings.* Only the *upper wing is swept;* single interplane strut and aileron transfer control bar, *fully rounded wing tips.* Also seen in two-seaters; separates from same-sized Christen Eagles by the asymmetry of the wings. See the similar Steen Skybolt (next entry) and note its less rounded wing tips.

Steen Skybolt

Length: 19' (5.79 m)   *Wingspan:* upper, 24' (7.32 m); lower, 23' (7.01 m)   *Cruising speed:* 130 mph (209 km/h)

Always a two-seater. *Upper wing swept, lower straight; very long-nosed, large rounded tail fin. Wing braces over the fuselage radiate from two points on the wing.* Compare the more conventional combination N braces on a Stolp Starduster. Sold as plans, with wing and fuselage kits available. More than 2500 kits have been sold.

Smith Miniplane

Length: 15'3" (4.65 m)   *Wingspan:* upper, 17' (5.18 m); lower, 15'9" (4.80 m)   *Cruising speed:* 118 mph (190 km/h)

Properly caled "mini." Small size; *wings not swept; lower wing slightly shorter; conventional N bracing.* The first models were known as DSA-1 (for Darn Small Airplane). Compare with the very similar EAA Biplane (next entry). EAAs tend to have a more streamlined engine cowling and a more upright tail fin.

EAA Biplane

Length: 17' (5.18 m)   *Wingspan:* both, 20' (6.10 m)   *Cruising speed:* 110 mph (177 km/h)

A small, single-seat with *unswept, equal-length wings* and conventional *N struts.* A subtle difference between the EAA Biplane and the Smith Miniplane is the way the lower wing appears to come out of the EAA fuselage; in the Smith Mini the fuselage appears to sit on top of the wing. The Smith Mini has a noticeably shorter lower wing.

EAA Acro-Sport, Acro-Sport II

Acro-Sport (single-seater) specifications: *Length:* 17'6" (5.33 m) *Wingspan:* upper, 19'7" (5.97 m); lower, 19'1" (5.82 m)   *Cruising speed:* 105 mph (169 km/h)

The only biplane illustrated here with *unswept wings of nearly equal length and a single streamlined strut, plus aileron control transfer bar.* Designed to be built from plans and construction manuals. More than 800 have been built and flown.

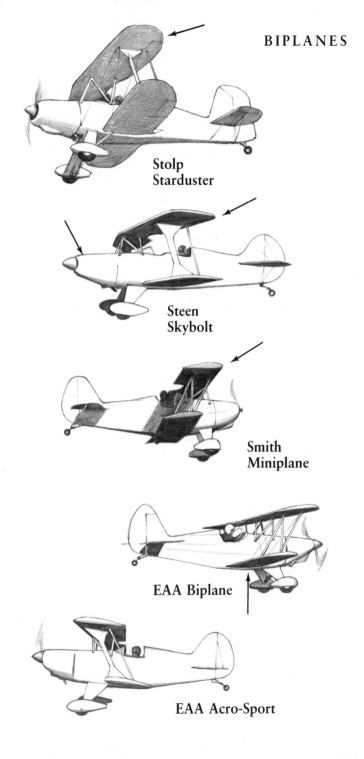

BIPLANES

Stolp
Starduster

Steen
Skybolt

Smith
Miniplane

EAA Biplane

EAA Acro-Sport

Eagle Aircraft Eagle 220, 300

Length: 27'6" (8.38 m)   *Wingspan:* 55' (16.76 m)   *Working speed:*
65–115 mph (105–185 km/h)

Not common. A 1981 introduction: *A biplane with extremely long, thin wings.* The typical agplane cockpit sits amid a maze of wires, struts, and braces; *large tail fin.*

A revival from the era when biplanes dominated the agricultural spraying industry, this Bellanca-designed agplane has an aspect totally different from the old biplanes converted to spraying: The wings are based on sailplane designs, long, thin, and tapering. More than 90 were produced by mid-1983. Earliest versions (not illustrated) used a radial engine, and the total length was only 26 feet (7.92 m). Last models produced were in-line pistons; model numbers (220, 300) indicate horsepower.

Schweizer (Grumman) Ag-Cat

Length: 25'7" (7.80 m)   *Wingspan:* 42'3" (12.88 m)   *Working speed:* 98 mph (158 km/h)

Separate this biplane-agplane from older biplanes converted to crop use by its *massive, high tail fin; all-metal skin; modern roll-bar cockpit; and trimmed speed-wing wing tips.*

The original Ag-Cat was designed by Grumman but never manufactured until Schweizer, a family-run designer of sailplanes, started manufacturing them under license from Grumman in 1957. Since 1981, Schweizer has been the sole owner of the design, now marketing an Ag-Cat B with a standard 600-horsepower radial engine. When one considers this class of agricultural planes — many (like the Schweizer) with pressurized cockpits to keep aerial sprays and dusts away from the pilot, air conditioning, and airframes meant to collapse slowly around a rigid cockpit in the case of a crash — one ceases to wonder why there are very few old, bold crop dusters. Compare these planes with the Call-Air A2 (next page) where the pilot simply put a barrel of pesticide in the passenger's seat and took off.

Schweizer Ag-Cat Super-B

Length: 24'5" (7.44 m)   *Wingspan:* 42'5" (12.93 m)   *Working speed:* 115 mph (185 km/h)

Very similar to the Schweizer/Grumman Ag-Cat when fitted with radial engine, but *the increased distance between the upper and lower wing is quite noticeable.* Even when fitted with a turbine engine (bottom sketch), it can't be confused with the Eagle (top of page) because of its shorter, broader wings and massive tail.

While the radial Super-Bs look like their Schweizer/Grumman ancestors (of which some 2000 fly worldwide), the small but visible change in the top wing, raising it 8 inches (20 cm), improved the plane's lift by decreasing wing-to-wing turbulence and enhanced the pilot's forward vision while diving, and upward vision in all attitudes.

AGRICULTURAL PLANES

**Eagle Aircraft
Eagle 300**

Schweizer Ag-Cat

Schweizer Ag-Cat Super-B

Call-Air A2, A5

Length: 23'5" (7.25 m)   *Wingspan:* 36' (11.11 m)   *Cruising speed:*
102 mph (164 km/h)

Extremely rare, and probably permanently parked in a quiet part
of the airfield. The *only production passenger aircraft with a low,
braced wing.* Wing is constant chord (width) with rounded tips;
three-strut landing gear usually has two struts covered with speed
pants. Compare with the Intermountain Call-Air A9 agricultural
plane (next entry).

Fewer than 50 built as passenger planes, a few more as Call-Air A5
and A6 crop dusters, with spray material carried inside the A2-style
cabin; included here because its use of the constant-chord wing with
high-lift qualities was unique when the plane was designed in 1939.
Built in Wyoming at an airfield with an elevation of 6200 feet, the
Call-Air was perfectly at home in "high and hot" thin air.

Intermountain Mfg. Co. Call-Air A9, Aero Commander, Sparrow, Quail, Snipe, AAM Thrush Commander

Length: 24' (7.32 m)   *Wingspan:* 35' (10.67 m)   *Working speed:*
100 mph (161 km/h)

Not so common as some agricultural planes, last produced in
Mexico by Aeronautica Agricola Mexicana. *Typical agplane shape,
low wing braced with three struts, equal-chord (width) wings, light
wire braces on tail planes, triple braces to forward wheels,* somewhat
old-fashioned *curved tail fin and tail planes.* A rare Snipe model has
a radial engine.

Agplane fans will see the family history of the Call-Air A9 in the
triple wing braces and triple wheel struts, picked up from the original
Call-Air A2 monoplane (above) and the now very rare Call-Air A5
and A6 agplanes. A Wyoming company developed the Call-Air A9
and manufactured a few hundred from 1963 to 1965. That design
was sold to Aero Commander (a division of Rockwell — later, North
American Rockwell). The A9 design survives today in the triple
braces to the front wheels in the Thrush agplanes, which have a modern unbraced wing. Rockwell sold off the braced-wing design to
Aeronautica Agricola Mexicana. A few of the earliest Call-Air A9s
did not have windows in the roof of the cockpit. Close at hand, note
the distinct droop to the leading edge of the wing, giving the plane a
very short takeoff roll (1200 feet) when fully loaded.

AGRICULTURAL PLANES

Call-Air A2, A5

Call-Air A9

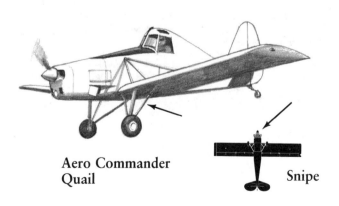

**Aero Commander
Quail**

Snipe

Piper PA25 Pawnee

Length: 24' (7.32 m)   *Wingspan:* 36'2" (11.02 m)   *Working speed:* 95 mph (153 km/h)

A small, old-fashioned-looking agplane is either a Pawnee or one of the Sparrow Commander/Call-Air A9 types; compare with them before deciding. *Low wing has a pair of braces on top, tail planes with paired braces top and bottom, wings are fabric over rib, and it usually shows up clearly, rounded wing tips, rounded tail geometry.*

One of the first pure agplanes; built between 1959 and 1982; early replacement for the old biplane dusters. The high placement of the pilot, the rear cockpit windows, and the extra-long nose for progressive collapse if crashed, plus interior safety features, were designed with the assistance of Cornell University agricultural and mechanical engineering studies.

Cessna Ag Truck, Ag Wagon, Ag Pickup, Ag Husky

Length: 25'3" (7.70 m)   *Wingspan:* 40'4" (12.30 m)   *Working speed:* variable, about 100 mph (161 km/h)

Quite variable window configurations, but always with these constants: *Wing is braced by a single, streamlined strut that is faired into the wing; unbraced tail planes; single, spring-steel struts to front wheels; very sharp (9-degree) dihedral that begins after the wing leaves the fuselage horizontally.*

Developed in 1965, the Cessna Ag series has a number of names signifying nothing more than varieties of engines, load-carrying capacity, and variations in windows — many early models before 1969 lacked the rear and top cockpit windows. A few models beginning in 1971 had high-lift drooped wing tips. All models (and other Cessna singles) since 1980 have the conical camber wing tips.

Piper PA36 Brave, Pawnee Brave, WTA New Brave 375, 400

Length: 27'6" (8.38 m)   *Wingspan:* 38'9" (11.83 m)   *Working speed:* 112 mph (180 km/h)

Typical agricultural low-wing monoplane. *Unbraced wings* (compare Thrush and Air Tractor, next entries); *wings of equal chord* (after fairing at wing root); *unbraced tail plane; forward landing gear struts are streamlined; shock absorbing; squared-off shape to tail fin, wing tips, and tail planes.*

Developed by Piper in 1972, once manufactured by WTA, Inc., a Texas company that also produced a Piper PA18 Super Cub. The extra-long nose of the Brave is so designed to collapse progressively in case of a crash. Not manufactured with radial engines or in two-seat models (compare the Thrush and Air Tractor).

AGRICULTURAL PLANES

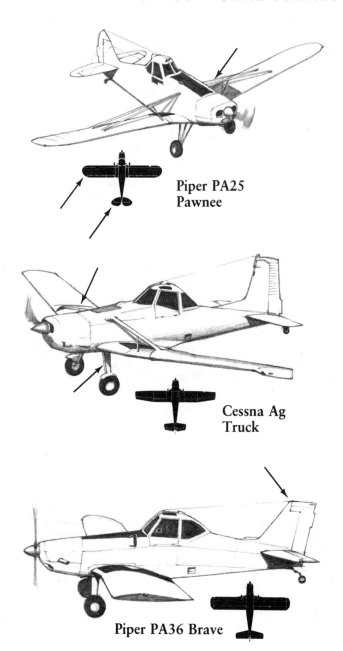

Piper PA25
Pawnee

Cessna Ag
Truck

Piper PA36 Brave

Ayres Thrush, Bull Thrush, Turbo Thrush, Rockwell-Commander Thrush

Length: 29'5" (8.96 m)   *Wingspan:* 44'5" (13.54 m)   *Working speed:* 110 mph (177 km/h)

Typical agricultural low-wing monoplane with *unbraced wings;* compare the Air Tractor (next entry) before deciding; *fixed gear; three struts for each forward wheel; pair of thin wire braces above and below tail planes; equal-chord (width) wings, with trapezoidal tips.*

Developed by Rockwell-Commander in 1965, manufactured by the Ayres Corporation after 1977. Comes in a variety of configurations, but all have the same field marks. The original models came with radial engines; recently with in-line turboprop engines (top picture). A two-seat cabin is standard on the 1200-horsepower radial Bull Thrush (bottom sketch), but is also available on the turboprop airframe. Bull Thrush carries up to 510 gallons of liquid spray.

Air Tractor 301, 401, 501, 400, 402, 502, 503

Length: 27' (8.23 m)   *Wingspan:* 45'1" (13.75 m)   *Working speed:* 130 mph (209 km/h)

Typical low-wing agricultural plane. *Unbraced wing,* compare the Thrush (previous entry) before deciding; *fixed gear, single, spring-steel strut carries each wheel; wing of equal chord (depth), with straight squared-off wing tips; pair of light braces on the underside only of the tail plane.*

Manufactured in various models since 1972. The field marks are consistent, although the plane is equipped with radial engines (model 301, lower sketch) or turboprop engines (model 302, 400, 402, 502); designed by Leland Snow, who also designed the Snow S2 agplanes, which became the Rockwell Thrush, now the Ayres Thrush. It is also manufactured in a two-seater (compare the Thrush).

Weatherly 620, 620TP, 201

Length: 27'3" (8.30 m)   *Wingspan:* 41' (12.5 m)   *Working speed:* 105 mph (169 km/h)

Not common, and quite variable. All models have *low, unbraced wing of constant chord (width); very strong dihedral begins a few feet out from fuselage; top of triangular tail fin is clipped.* An option is detachable vanes that extend the spray path by about 8 feet (2.47 m).

Weatherly Aviation began by converting Fairchild M62s (page 22) to crop sprayers, and continued with their own modifications of that design. Except for the radial engines on some models (bottom sketch) the plane has an air of angularity about it that is unique, including the constant-chord wings, the delta tail fin, and the trapezoidal tail planes. Even the tapers in the fuselage section appear to be flat sections.

AGRIGULTURAL PLANES

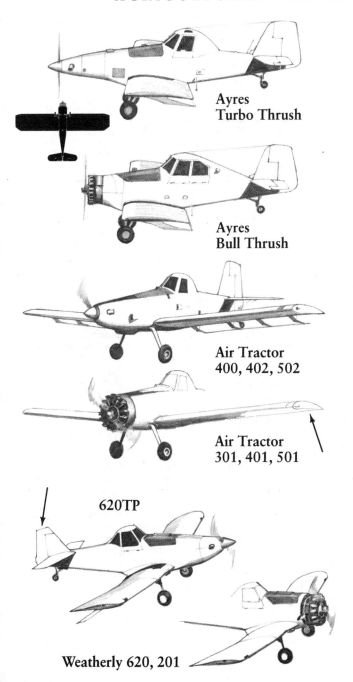

Ayres
Turbo Thrush

Ayres
Bull Thrush

Air Tractor
400, 402, 502

Air Tractor
301, 401, 501

620TP

Weatherly 620, 201

Ryan ST3 (PT-21, PT-22 NR-1), Ryan ST

Length: 22'5" (6.83 m)   *Wingspan:* 30'1" (9.18 m)   *Cruising speed:* 123 mph (198 km/h)

Quite rare. *Constant-chord* (width) *low wing; rounded tips;* both the wings and tail planes are braced, top and bottom, with wire; *cylinder heads of the standard engine project through cowling; distinct, abrupt turtleback to rear cockpit.*

Of the thousands built, more than 500 PT-21s survived WWII training duties and entered the civilian market. Although slow, the plane was more than strong enough for acrobatics (the point of the noisy wire bracing). The plane had a fairly high stall speed, 64 mph (103 km/h), and sank like a rock without power. The civil version (ST) had an in-line engine and wheel pants (see sketch); the military five-banger was easier to work on, and the wheel pants were dropped in deference to the abuse landing gears took from student pilots.

Fairchild PT-19 (M62), Cornell

Length: 27'8" (8.5 m)   *Wingspan:* 35'11" (11 m)   *Cruising speed:* 120 mph (193 km/h)

Rare old birds. *Unbraced low wing; twin tandem cockpits* (which may be enclosed in a greenhouse, top sketch); *fixed tail-dragger landing gear without wheel pants.*

Built by the thousands; a largely wood spar and plywood exterior basic trainer flown by nearly a million WWII student pilots. Faster and sturdier than the biplanes of that era. When fitted with radial engines, known as the PT-23 — a much less common type than the PT-19. Greenhouse canopy supplied on Canadian Air Force versions (the Cornell) and on the few civilian models, designated M62. All were remarkably durable (although the wood construction has created problems after the passage of nearly 50 years) and regarded as forgiving and easy to fly.

Consolidated Vultee Valiant, BT-13, BT-15, SNV-1

Length: 28'7" (8.65 m)   *Wingspan:* 42' (12.8 m)   *Cruising speed:* 170 mph (274 km/h)

Quite rare, although 10,000 built through WWII. An odd combination: *fully enclosed radial engine and large fixed tail-dragging gear* (the somewhat similar T-6 is a retractable tail dragger, page 47). *Tall, narrow tail fin.*

Vultee developed the basic trainer BT-13 before merging with Consolidated and built them through WWII; they were still in military service as late as 1950. Known to a generation of pilots as "the Vibrator" — more a reference to what it did to airport windows than what it did to the pilots. Of the thousands that went on the war surplus market, most were cannibalized — the Valiant's Wasp Junior radial engine fit the Stearman Kaydet, a popular sportster and crop duster.

LOW-WING SINGLES

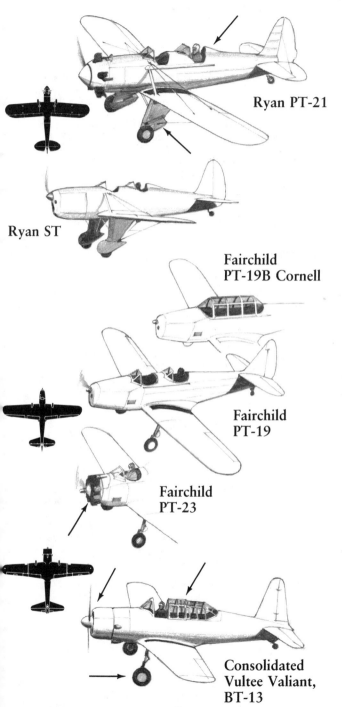

Ryan PT-21

Ryan ST

Fairchild
PT-19B Cornell

Fairchild
PT-19

Fairchild
PT-23

Consolidated
Vultee Valiant,
BT-13

de Havilland DHC1 Chipmunk

Length: 25'5" (7.75 m)   *Wingspan:* 34'4" (10.46 m)   *Cruising speed:* 124 mph (200 km/h)

Rare in the U.S., more common in Canada. *Unbraced low wing; fixed tail-dragging gear.* Compared to the Fairchild PT-19 Cornell, the Chipmunk has a *short, two-pane greenhouse canopy* that sits much farther back than the Fairchild's. A large air intake sits under the propeller spinner and is offset sharply to the port side of the aircraft.

Created in Canada to replace the biplane DH82 Tiger Moth as a primary trainer, the Chipmunk was built from 1946 to 1953 in Canada and Great Britain. It is the most antique looking of all the post–WWII all-metal construction aircraft. If you have a chance to see one near a Gipsy Moth or a Tiger Moth, note the similarity in the slimness of the fuselage and the shape of the engine cowling — the Chipmunk is very much a one-winged Moth.

Varga Kachina, Morrisey 2000

Length: 21'2" (6.45 m)   *Wingspan:* 30' (9.14 m)   *Cruising speed:* 127 mph (204 km/h)

A *small, low-wing single,* of modern all-metal construction, but with an *old-fashioned-looking "fighter" cockpit canopy* that covers tandem seating; *near constant-chord* (width) *wings with rounded tips; upright tail fin.*

A design created in wood and fabric construction by William Morrisey, a Douglas test pilot, after WWII. Known then as the Morrisey Nifty. Redesigned in all metal in the 1960s. Many sold with *tail-dragging* gear, to appeal to the owner who wants to increase the illusion that he's flying a WWII fighter plane. Built standard with dual controls; a popular sport and training aircraft, particularly for the weekend rental market. Morrisey has reacquired the design.

Gulfstream American Yankee,
T-Cat, Lynx, AA-1, AA-5 Cheetah, AG5B Tiger

Length: 19'3" (5.86 m)   *Wingspan:* 24'5" (7.45 m)   *Cruising speed:* 135 mph (217 km/h)

A series of fairly common *unbraced low-wing, fixed tricycle gear two-seaters.* The *constant-chord* (width) *wings have a strong dihedral, and small fillet-fairings* on both edges at the wing root; *bubble canopy* plus *small side window.*

Created by noted small-plane designer Jim Bede using modern honeycomb and metal-to-metal bonded construction. Built by Bede Aviation in 1972; then American Aviation; then by Grumman American; finally by Gulfstream American, until 1978. The model illustrated is the Lynx, with wheel pants. There were models built with standard dual controls for primary training. Lower drawing of four-place Gulfstream American Cheetah, a stretched Lynx with a conventional cockpit canopy. Now produced (AG5B) by American General Aircraft.

LOW-WING SINGLES

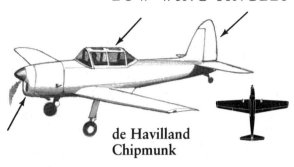

de Havilland
Chipmunk

Varga Kachina,
Morrisey 2000

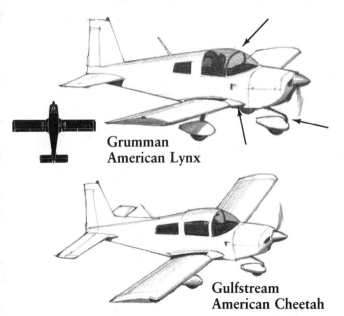

Grumman
American Lynx

Gulfstream
American Cheetah

Beech Skipper 77

Length: 24' (7.32 m) *Wingspan:* 30' (9.14 m) *Cruising speed:* 112 mph (180 km/h)

Uncommon fixed-gear trainer. Compare with Piper Tomahawk before deciding. Skipper has *Hershey-bar wing* (with fillet-fairing to leading edge) *and tail plane, true T-tail; trapezoidal side window in each door;* shorter and wider wings than the Piper Tomahawk. Skipper *main landing gear is spraddle-legged,* leaning back and out, giving the plane a very wide stance on the runway.

In use by 1979, a year after the competitive Tomahawk. The primary trainer for company-franchised Beech Aero Centers. Originally planned as a conventional-tail aircraft and so flown as a prototype in 1978; the T-tail was apparently triggered by the success of the Tomahawk in 1978.

Piper PA38 Tomahawk

Length: 23'1" (7.03 m) *Wingspan:* 34' (10.36 m) *Cruising speed:* 114 mph (183 km/h)

Very common trainer. *Pure Hershey-bar wing and tail plane without any fillets or fairings.* Wing is visibly longer and slimmer than on comparable Beech Skipper; *not quite a T-tail* (a cross-tail); *rectangular window in each door.*

Piper's very successful entrant into the modern trainer market, more than 1000 ordered in the first year (1978). Achieves the same wide stance as the Skipper (for better runway control) but without the spraddle-legged look. Tomahawk's 4-foot 9-inch wheelbase was achieved by wing-mounting the main gear; Skipper's 5-foot 2-inch wheelbase requires longer wheel struts since it arises at the root of the wing and fuselage.

Ercoupe (Alon Aircoupe, Mooney M10 Cadet)

Length: 20'9" (6.32 m) *Wingspan:* 30' (9.14 m) *Cruising speed:* 110 mph (177 km/h)

Increasingly rare. *Distinctive twin fin tail* is unique on single-engine aircraft; *strong dihedral in constant-chord* (width) *wings; rounded wing tips.*

Designed and first built just before WWII, the Ercoupe was intended as a plane for Sunday drivers, and survived until 1970 (Mooney M10 Cadet). Used a conventional steering wheel that moved the ailerons and rudder simultaneously for turning; angle of climb and descent governed normally, by pushing or pulling on the "steering column" stick. It's designed to be spin and stall proof, if not idiot proof. Ercoupe also introduced the tricycle landing gear to the private pilot, making it astonishingly easy to fly off the runway. The lack of foot pedals made flying accessible to many handicapped pilots. (It looked so easy that the author's father talked of buying one — until the author's mother overheard him.)

LOW-WING SINGLES

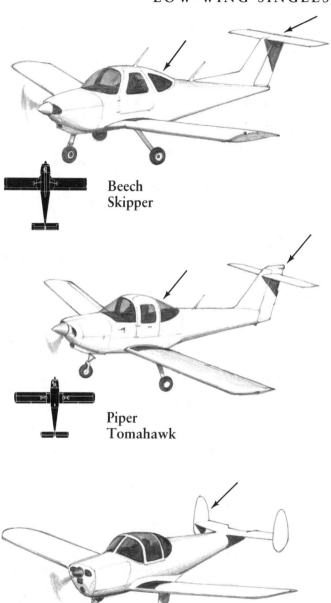

Beech
Skipper

Piper
Tomahawk

Ercoupe

Beech Sierra (retractable), Sundowner, Sport, Musketeer

Length: 25'9" (7.85 m)   *Wingspan:* 32'9" (9.98 m)   *Cruising speed:* 158 mph (254 km/h)

All models quite common. Top drawing: Sierra. *Retractable gear folds outward; wheels remain visible under wing; long, thin, rectangular tail plane; perfectly rectangular wings enter fuselage without any fairing.* A distinct field mark, when you have other similarly sized airplanes to compare with it, is the *high cockpit ceiling.* All two-window versions seat three; those with three or four side windows seat five, including the pilot.

Developed in 1969 as a retractable-gear Musketeer; marketed after 1970 as the Sierra. Early versions were regarded as slow and klutzy. Major changes included increased engine power (from 170 to 200 hp) and aerodynamic fairings underwing to shield the retracted wheels — the so-called speed bumps. Still not a high-performance aircraft, but it's roomy inside, with unusually good pilot visibility.

Middle drawing: Musketeer II. No longer manufactured. Wings and tail surfaces are identical to Sierra, but with fixed gear. Oldest models of Musketeer have two side windows.

Bottom drawing: Sundowner also discontinued. Distinguish from other fixed-gear Musketeer types by the larger side windows (note rear window in particular) and the longer propeller spinner and slightly more streamlined engine cowling. A two-window version, with same large spinner and streamline cowling, is the Sport.

Aerospatiale (SOCATA) Rallye

Length: 23'9" (7.24 m)   *Wingspan:* 31'6" (9.61 m)   *Cruising speed:* 108 mph (174 km/h)

Rare low-wing with fixed tricycle gear; large one-piece side window on glass canopy; wing and tail plane are constant chord (width). When in view, note the substantial *bullet-shaped "close-out" fairing* at the tail end of the fuselage.

A variable series of small planes with two-, three-, and four-seat versions, built in France since 1958. Various names for different models — Sport, Tourisme, Club, and Minerva. It's been imported into the U.S. and Canada since 1974; the most common model is the 225-horsepower Minerva. The Hershey-bar wing and tail plane resembles certain Piper models, and, curiously, Piper was the U.S. importer in the 1970s.

Mudry C.A.P. 10

Length: 23'6" (7.16 m)   *Wingspan:* 26'5" (8.06 m)   *Cruising speed:* 155 mph (250 km/h)

Distinctive little *Spitfire-shaped* plane with an apparently *oversized bubble canopy.* Rare in the United States, but flown by some flight-instruction programs, and thus common locally.

The Mudry is probably the best example of the decline and fall of the U.S. light-plane industry in the face of high premiums for product liability insurance. No one's making a little, inexpensive, side-by-side aerobatic plane for advanced *civilian* pilot training, so this French import (first flown in 1970), based on the old home-built Piel Emeraude, is being imported in the 1990s.

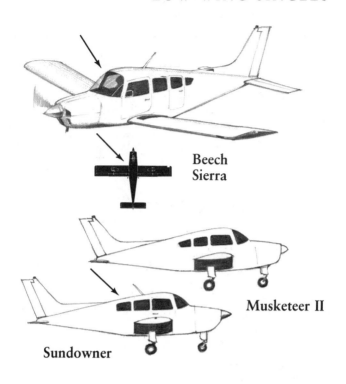

Beech
Sierra

Musketeer II

Sundowner

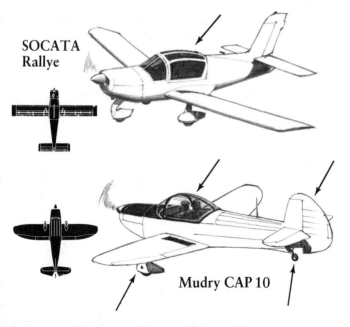

SOCATA
Rallye

Mudry CAP 10

Piper PA28-180R Cherokee Arrow, Arrow II, Arrow III

Length: 24'2" (7.37 m)   *Wingspan:* 32' (9.75 m)   *Cruising speed:* 162 mph (261 km/h)

Less common than the nonretractable Cherokee series. *Identical to the fixed-gear Cherokees* (see the Piper PA28 Cherokee and Cherokee Warrior field notes, below). For simplicity's sake: The Arrow II (illustrated) has three side windows and constant-chord wings; a two-window Arrow is a I. The Arrow III has the new, tapered Piper wing and is identical to the Cherokee Warrior II with tapered wings, except for its retractable gear. There are a few Arrow IIIs with turbocharged engines (see bottom sketch next to Arrow IV, page 33, showing the turbocharger air scoop). On the flight line with wheels down, an Arrow is a *Cherokee without wheel pants.* On the air traffic controller's radio, they're all just plain Cherokees.

Piper PA28 Cherokee 140, 150, 160, Charger, Flite-Liner

Length: 23'3" (7.08 m)   *Wingspan:* 30' (9.14 m)   *Cruising speed:* with 180-horsepower engine, 130 mph (209 km/h)

Common. *Small four-seater, candy-bar wing, fixed tricycle gear with wheel pants.*

Introduced in 1961, superseded by the Cherokee Warrior in 1974, when it received the multi-angled "new Piper" wing. Engines built with 140 to 235 horsepower. The plane was eventually designated Charger. When stretched to hold six, it became the Cherokee SIX (page 32). The 150-horsepower version, designated Flite-Liner, was a popular club plane and trainer in the 1970s. The original Cherokee introduced considerable use of simple curves and fiberglass and plastic construction to the small-plane market.

Piper PA28 Cherokee Warrior, Warrior II, Cadet

Length: 23'9" (7.25 m)   *Wingspan:* 35' (10.67 m)   *Cruising speed:* 135 mph (217 km/h)

Common. *Fixed tricycle gear; dihedral in wing, none in tail; three side windows.* Wing is of complicated geometry: leaves fuselage *with fairing to leading edge; short equal-span section; leading and trailing edges taper to tip at unequal angles. Tail plane a pure Hershey-bar rectangle.*

Flown since 1974, the first Piper to abandon their trademark of constant-chord (width) wing plans. Sold under various names with slight differences, including engine horsepower: Cherokee Warrior, renamed Warrior II (160 hp), Dakota (235 hp), Archer II (180 hp). All versions seat four, including the pilot. "Cadet," a trainer, drops third side window and, like most bouncing trainers, the wheel pants.

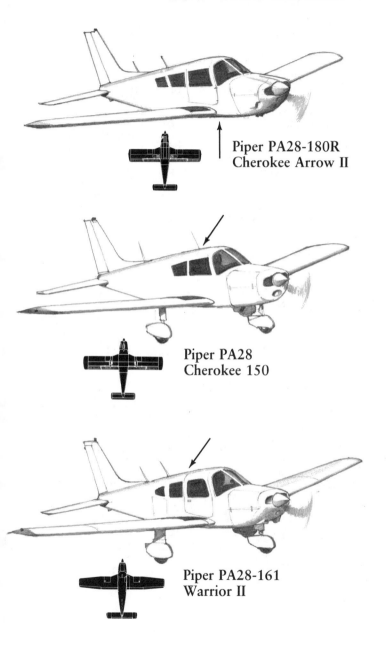

Piper PA28-180R
Cherokee Arrow II

Piper PA28
Cherokee 150

Piper PA28-161
Warrior II

Piper PA32 Cherokee SIX, PA32R-300 Lance, PA32RT-300 Lance II

Length: 27'9" (8.45 m)   *Wingspan:* 32'9" (9.95 m)   *Cruising speed:* 158 mph (254 km/h)

A common, *large, fixed-gear airplane.* Typical early Piper wing — a Hershey-bar rectangle with fairing to leading edge; *an oversized Cherokee with four side windows.* The earliest models had four squared windows, not the variable geometrical shapes seen in the sketch. A retractable Cherokee SIX, with Hershey-bar wings, is a Lance, of which a few models had T-tails (upper sketch).

Carrying six, including the pilot, for many years (1964–1979) it was Piper's largest single-engine and the largest fixed-gear single in the private aviation field. When equipped with an optional 300-horsepower engine, it's suitable for use on skis or floats. Occasionally used as an air ambulance or short-haul freighter; then equipped with a single large door at the rear of the cabin that folds up. Last produced in 1979, when Piper replaced it with the non-retractable PA32 Saratoga, using the longer, tapered, "new Piper" wing plan.

Piper PA32R-301 Saratoga

Length: 28'4" (8.64 m)   *Wingspan:* 36'2" (11.02 m)   *Cruising speed:* 162 mph (261 km/h)

What we have here is a *Cherokee SIX with the new, tapered Piper wing.* If you can't get a look at the wing, call it a Cherokee.

The Saratoga is a six-passenger addition, usually sold with retractable gear, many with turbocharged engines (see sketch under main drawing). The Saratoga basically replaced the Cherokee SIX and the T-tailed Lance; first produced in 1979. The name change signifies mostly the wing change, plus more horsepower.

Piper PA28RT Arrow IV

Length: 27' (8.23 m)   *Wingspan:* 35'5" (10.80 m)   *Cruising speed:* 165 mph (265 km/h)

Not especially common. What we have here is *a Cherokee Warrior II with a T-tail.* Has the *tapered wings of the Warrior series* (page 30). A much larger plane than the little T-tailed Beech Skipper; fully retractable gear.

If there was ever any proof that the T-tail had some sales advantages, as opposed to utilitarian purpose, it was sticking one on the old reliable Cherokee Warrior II/Archer airframes in 1977. The T-tail Arrow IV came in conventional and turbocharged models, as did the Arrow III (see bottom sketch showing air intake).

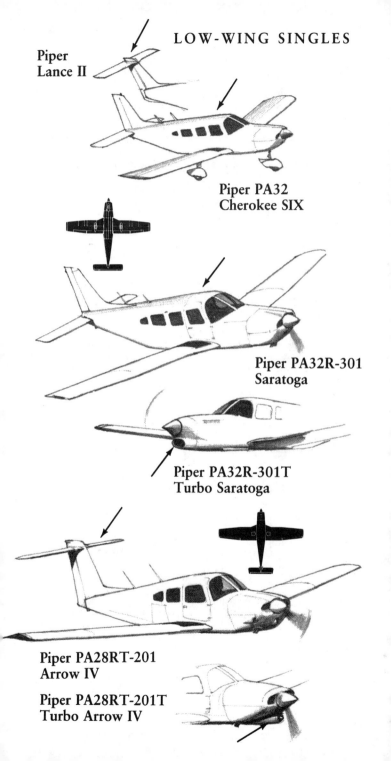

LOW-WING SINGLES

Piper
Lance II

Piper PA32
Cherokee SIX

Piper PA32R-301
Saratoga

Piper PA32R-301T
Turbo Saratoga

Piper PA28RT-201
Arrow IV

Piper PA28RT-201T
Turbo Arrow IV

Beech Bonanza 35, F33A

Length: 26'5" (8.05 m)   *Wingspan:* 33'6" (10.21 m)   *Cruising speed:* 190 mph (306 km/h)

Anything with a *V-tail* is a Bonanza 35. Confusion is generated by two conventional-tail aircraft, the Bonanza A36 (next entry) and the Bonanza 33, which is identical to the Bonanza 35 except that it has a conventional tail. (See the Bonanza 36 entry for details.)

Built from 1947 to date, more than 10,000 are flying in North America. About 1200 were built with only two side windows, before 1961; however, some owners have added the third side window to their own pre-1961 aircraft. It comes with a variety of engines, including turbocharging. Early models had a smaller tail surface, less steeply angled, but after-market modifications have been made to most of those. Of all-metal construction since its inception.

Beech Bonanza A36

Length: 27'6" (8.38 m)   *Wingspan:* 33'6" (10.21 m)   *Cruising speed:* 188 mph (302 km/h)

Commonest of the large, single-engine, retractable-gear planes. *Fairing from fuselage to wing's leading edge; four side windows; large doors on starboard side.* If you take the Beech 35, above, and put a Beech 36 conventional tail on it, you have the Beech Bonanza 33 (once known as the Debonair).

Built since 1968, it seats six, including the pilot; for many years, the only six-passenger, retractable-gear single. Turbocharged model (illustrated) shows intake and cooling louvers on engine cowling. The smaller Debonair/Bonanza 33 has three side windows and seats four, including the pilot. Since 1982, the turbocharged model has a 37-foot 6-inch (11.43 m) wingspan. A few turboprop conversions, with wing tip-tanks, have been made.

North American Rockwell
Commander 111, 112, 114

Length: 25' (7.62 m)   *Wingspan:* 32'11" (10.04 m)   *Cruising speed:* 157 mph (253 km/h)

Not common. Best field mark for this low-wing single is the *tail plane, mounted midway up the tail fin.* Overhead, the *wing leading edge is straight, at right angles to the centerline,* except for the noticeable fairing from fuselage to leading edge; strong (7-degree) dihedral in wing, none in tail plane; a wide, chubby look to the cabin area.

Built since 1971, it's a high-performance, four-seat single. The unusual tail design caused some difficulty at first, including the loss of a prototype, and the requirement to redesign the rear fuselage and tail assembly. The interior cabin space is unusually wide for a four-passenger single and gives the aircraft its look of being bulky forward and over the wing. With a three-bladed prop, it's a Commander Aircraft 114B.

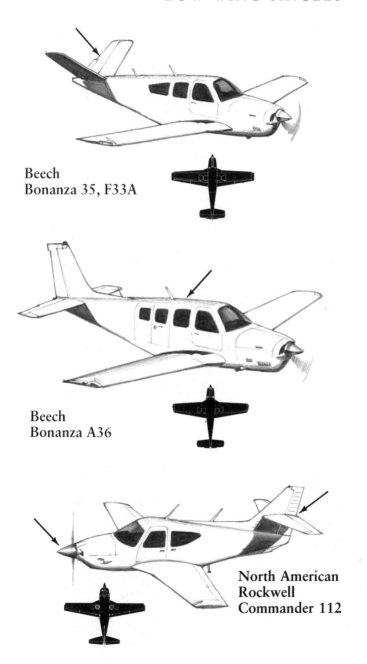

Beech
Bonanza 35, F33A

Beech
Bonanza A36

North American
Rockwell
Commander 112

Piper PA24 Comanche

Length: 25' (7.62 m)   *Wingspan:* 36' (10.98 m)   *Cruising speed:* 182 mph (293 km/h)

Chunky fuselage; commonly, two side windows, last models had three; retractable gear is visible, tucked in against fuselage; Beech Bonanza–type wing, fairing to a straight leading edge, tapered trailing edge.

Piper's first low-wing was also its first retractable. The wing appears to be a Beech borrow, but is in fact a U.S. government design — several thousand were built before production ended in 1972. For the last few years, the plane stretched the cabin to seat five or six and added the third window, at which point Piper shifted to the Arrow series (page 30) as the standard six-passenger retractable.

TBM 700

Length: 34'2" (12.16 m)   *Wingspan:* 39'11" (12.16 m)   *Cruising speed:* 345 mph (555 km/h)

Longer, slimmer, shorter span than the Piper Malibu (above), which it somewhat resembles. *Long-nosed, airscoop below small four-bladed propeller, engine exhaust visible starboard, noticeable dihedral in horizontal stabilizer, odd "bent-down" pilot's side window.*

A successful 1989 introduction, as American manufacturers concentrated on corporate pure jets, Mooney and SOCATA (France) combined to produce this pressurized, 30,000-foot-ceiling turboprop business aircraft. Its cruising speed and rate of climb, 2303 feet (702 m) per minute, puts it nearly in jet performance, while its low stall speed of 71 mph (113 km/h) makes it amenable to small airports and noise-restricted areas.

Piper PA46 Malibu

Length: 28'4" (8.63 m)   *Wingspan:* 43' (13.11 m)   *Cruising speed:* estimated, 230 mph (370 km/h)

New in 1983. Marked by *a heavy look to the fuselage; long, thin wings.*

The Malibu, which is turbocharged and pressurized, can operate to 25,000 feet. The cabin is unusually large for a single (4 feet by 4 feet, interior dimensions) and does not taper from the forward to the rear seats — note the field mark of a rotund fuselage. The wing design is quite unusual for a commercial aircraft: The ratio of wing length to width (chord) is 11 to 1 (most business-style aircraft ratios are about 7 to 1). It seats six, including the crew.

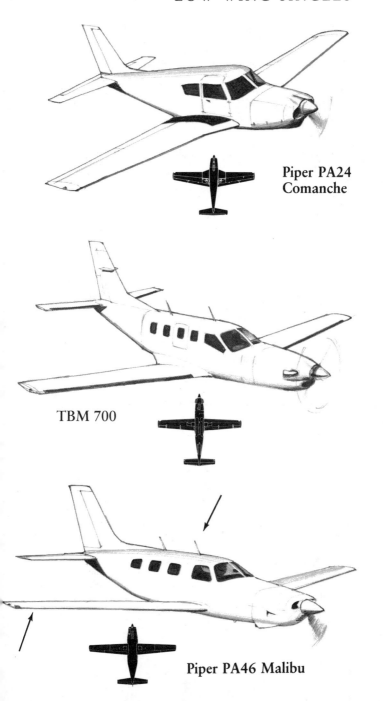

Piper PA24
Comanche

TBM 700

Piper PA46 Malibu

Mooney Aircraft Corporation (briefly, Aerostar)

A series of four-place, tricycle-gear aircraft with common field marks. *All leading edges — wing, tail fin, and tail plane — are straight lines, at right angles to the centerline of the airplane. All trailing surfaces angle forward;* gives the planes the image of leaning forward into the air. *Compare the small, tail-dragging Mooney Mite* (page 46).

Mooney M20, 201MSE (top drawing), 205, 231, 252, PFM (sketch)

201MSE specifications: *Length:* 24′8″ (7.52 m)   *Wingspan:* 36′1″ (10.67 m)   *Cruising speed:* 167 mph (269 km/h)

Current model has rounded-off side windows; earlier 201, 231, 205 with square-edged windows. Porsche-engined high-performance PFM (sketch) and a turboprop 231 have longer, sleeker engine cowlings; 205 has fully enclosed landing gear.

Mooney M20 Chapparal

Length: 23′2″ (7.06 m)   *Wingspan:* 35′ (10.67 m)   *Cruising speed:* 172 mph (277 km/h)

A series of very similar Mooneys, various engines and names, including Executive 21, Chapparal, and Super 21. There are some aerodynamically important streamlining details, but none really visible. The most recent version, the Ranger (not illustrated), has fully covered wheel wells and lacks the dorsal fin fairing to the tail fin.

Planes built from 1969 to 1972 had the buttonhook tail (see sketch).

Mooney M22 Mustang

Length: 26′10″ (8.18 m)   *Wingspan:* 35′ (10.67 m)   *Cruising speed:* 214 mph (344 km/h)

Rare, built only from 1967 to 1969. *Pressurized,* which shows in the window design; *four small side windows — three square, trailing window round.* A very high performance single, with a 24,000-foot operating ceiling.

Mooney M20D Master, and Mark 21

Length: 23′2″ (7.06 m)   *Wingspan:* 35′ (10.67 m)   *Cruising speeds:* 130–150 mph (209–241 km/h)

The original production all-metal Mooneys. The Mooney M20D Master has *fixed tricycle gear, but lacks typical dorsal fin fairing to tail.* The Mooney Master, with retractable gear, grew up into the Mooney Ranger.

The Mooney M20C (last drawing), with retractable gear, would grow into the Mark 21 and be the parent of the Chapparal, Mark 201, and Mark 231 Mooneys. It has the dorsal fin. Both these early four-place Mooneys show a *distinct air-intake "chin"* below the propeller spinner.

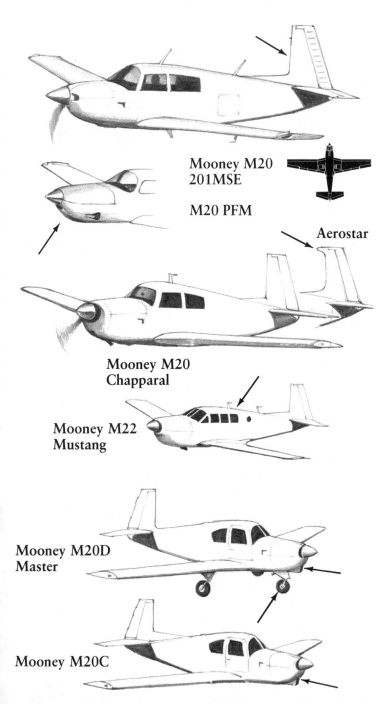

LOW-WING SINGLES

Mooney M20
201MSE

M20 PFM

Aerostar

Mooney M20
Chapparal

Mooney M22
Mustang

Mooney M20D
Master

Mooney M20C

SOCATA TB 20/21 Trinidad, TB 9 Tampico, TB 10 Tobago

Trinidad 20 specifications: *Length:* 25' (7.63 m)   *Wingspan:* 32' (9.76 m)   *Cruising speed:* 219 mph (352 km/h)

At first glance, resembles some Piper low-wing singles with constant-chord wings, but note the *sharp, erect vertical stabilizer, belly strakes just aft of wing root, designer-modern windows.* On the ground, *the gull-wing passenger door on each side is unique.*

With most American manufacturers deserting the trainer-sport field, the fixed-gear Tampico Club (sketch) is the most popular new plane of the decade, and the Trinidad and Tobago (a Trinidad with fixed gear and wheel fairings) are increasingly common in the United States.

SIAI-Marchetti S.205, S.208

S.205 specifications: *Length:* 26'3" (8 m)   *Wingspan:* 35'7" (10.86 m)   *Cruising speed:* 140 mph (226 km/h)

One of the few singles with a *typical cabin and wing tip-tanks* (see Navion, next page), but not all models delivered with tip-tanks! Most (but not all) U.S.-based planes have *retractable gear; the nose wheel remains visible.* Perhaps the best field mark is the *very upright tail; forward edge leans back; trailing edge is vertical; distinct dorsal fairing to tail.* What it looks like is a Mooney vertical stabilizer installed backwards.

Extremely variable, these SIAI 205s and 208s, with horsepowers from 180 (S.205-18) to 260 (S.208), and cruising speeds from pokey to fast. Most carry a pilot and three passengers.

SIAI-Marchetti SF.260

Length: 23' (7.02 m)   *Wingspan:* 27' (8.25 m)   *Cruising speed:* 214 mph (345 km/h)

The most fighter-plane-looking modern production aircraft, with *a sliding bubble canopy and always with tip-tanks; fairing to vertical stabilizer begins just aft of canopy.*

With a standard price approaching $200,000, this is the Lamborghini of personal aircraft. Used in Europe for advanced pilot training, and attempts have been made to sell it to the U.S. Air Force as a primary trainer. New, it can catch most recreational rebuilt World War II fighters. Fully aerobatic.

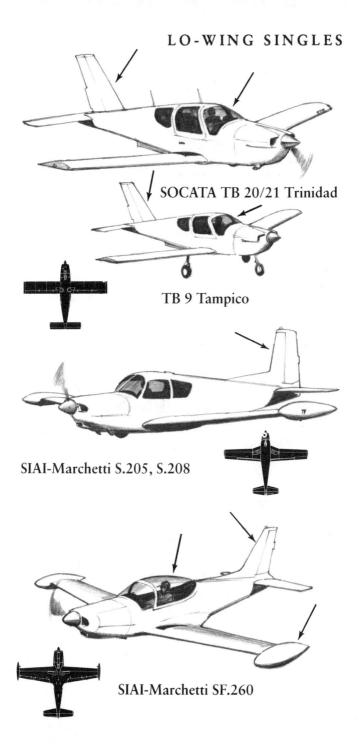

LO-WING SINGLES

SOCATA TB 20/21 Trinidad

TB 9 Tampico

SIAI-Marchetti S.205, S.208

SIAI-Marchetti SF.260

Navion Rangemaster

Length: 27′6″ (8.38 m)   *Wingspan:* 34′9″ (10.59 m)   *Cruising speed:* 290 mph (467 km/h)

A rare, odd bird: a *low-wing single with tip-tanks*. It's essentially similar in wing and tail configuration to the Ryan Navion, but with a built-up five-passenger cabin and automobile-type door on the port side of the aircraft.

A Texas aircraft parts manufacture picked up the old Ryan Navion design, spare parts, and tools to manufacture the Rangemaster — all quite similar except for the cabin, and supplied with a variety of engines. Like the prototype, it comes standard with dual controls.

Ryan Navion (L-17), North American Navion

Length: 27′8″ (8.43 m)   *Wingspan:* 33′5″ (10.18 m)   *Cruising speed:* 155 mph (249 km/h)

Rare. A low-wing single with a *bulbous cockpit canopy and slender rear fuselage. Nose wheel is visible* when tricycle gear is retracted. Could easily be confused with the even rarer Aero Commander 200 (next entry): *Navion's rear side window tapers sharply; two-piece windshield with noticeable center strip,* whereas the Aero Commander has a much larger rear window that sweeps up, and a one-piece windshield.

Manufactured in the late 1940s through 1951, it seats four, including the pilot. Ryan built hundreds of low-wing trainers during WWII, but purchased the Navion design from North American. Came standard with dual controls and a bench seat for two more passengers. Canopy slides back for access to cabin. Ryan added landing gear doors and personal comfort items to the basic North American design.

Aero Commander 200 (Meyers 200)

Length: 24′4″ (7.42 m)   *Wingspan:* 30′6″ (9.29 m)   *Cruising speed:* 215 mph (346 km/h)

Quite rare. A small *retractable tricycle gear,* distinguished by a *high cabin canopy,* automobile-type door on starboard side of the cabin. *Appearance is short-winged, slim-fuselaged,* aft of *bulbous canopy.* Could be confused with the Ryan Navion.

Aero Commander took over the Meyers 200, buying a design that put them in the high-performance, four-seat, retractable market in 1965. Very few Meyers 200s and not many more (perhaps 100) Aero Commander 200s were built from 1965 to 1967. Built with various engines, including one type with a turboprop, the Interceptor 400, with cruising speeds near 300 mph. More fun to fly than practical.

LOW-WING SINGLES

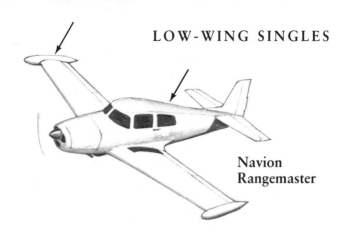

**Navion
Rangemaster**

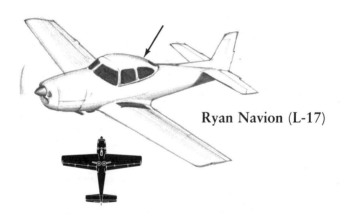

Ryan Navion (L-17)

Aero Commander 200

Temco (Globe) Swift 125

Length: 20'11" (6.38 m)   *Wingspan:* 29'4" (8.94 m)   *Cruising speed:* 140 mph (225 km/h)

Rare. A *small retractable, low-wing;* cockpit and windows varied, not good field marks; *strong* (8-degree) *dihedral in tail plane and wings* — very unusual in small singles and a distinct field mark at any altitude or attitude. Close at hand, a *unique engine grill,* like something from a 1950s General Motors automobile.

A few hundred of these 1945–1951 airplanes survive. They came standard with dual controls, some with all-Plexiglas canopy, some with enclosed cabin. Along with the Mooney Mite, one of the first post–WWII airplanes to take advantage of the wind-tunnel-tested wing designs of the National Advisory Committee on Aeronautics (NACA), precursor of NASA. Many fly today with much more powerful engines than the original 125 horsepower.

Bellanca Viking (and Cruisemaster 14193C)

Length: 26'4" (8.02 m)   *Wingspan:* 34'2" (10.41 m)   *Cruising speed:* 185 mph (298 km/h)

A small low-wing; *large strongly swept tail fin; strut under tail planes; dihedral in wing, none in tail plane; wraparound windshield; two large side windows; nose wheel does not retract fully, main gear carried in underwing fairings.*

Bellanca essentially took the Cruisemaster (next entry), added a tricycle gear, and dropped the outboard fins on the tail planes to make the Cruisemaster 14193. The swept tail fin was added in 1958, the name changed to Viking in 1966. No longer manufactured, although efforts are occasionally made to reintroduce it. Constructed of fabric over plywood and tubing.

Bellanca Cruisemaster, Cruiseair

Cruisemaster specifications: *Length:* 22'11" (7 m)   *Wingspan:* 34'2" (10.41 m)   *Cruising speed:* 180 mph (290 km/h)

Rare. *A stubby low-wing tail-dragger; main gear remains exposed when retracted; triple-tailed; central tail fin much larger than outboard fins; wire braces on tail plane; two side windows.*

About 100 Cruisemasters and a few hundred very similar Cruiseairs (smaller engines) were built from 1946 to 1958. Plane combined relatively high operating speeds with low landing speeds and a stall speed of about 50 mph. Highly regarded for sport use. Seats three or four, including the pilot. Construction is fabric over plywood.

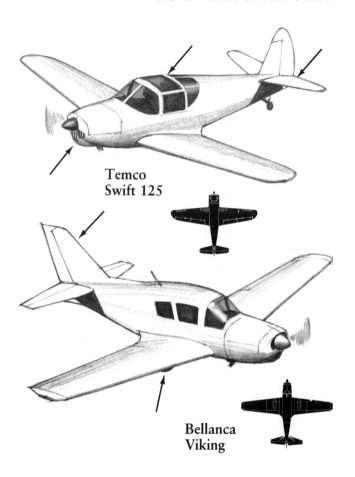

Temco
Swift 125

Bellanca
Viking

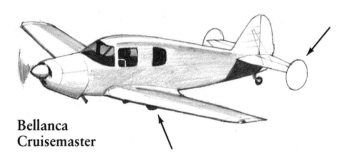

Bellanca
Cruisemaster

Mooney M18 Mite

Length: 18' (5.48 m)   *Wingspan:* 26'10" (8.20 m)   *Cruising speed:*
80 mph (129 km/h)

Rare. A classic Mooney design. Though *tiny, a one-seater,* it has
same wing and tail surface pattern as the four-seat Mooneys — *leading edges of wing and tail surfaces are a straight line at right angles
to the centerline of the fuselage.*
Built from 1947 to 1954, the Mooney Mite was a favorite sport
plane for ex-fighter pilots — inexpensive to own, cheap to fly — but
it did not answer the needs of the family-oriented pilot. Originally
designed to use the old Crosley automobile engine, the last models
(M18) had a regulation 65-horsepower aircraft engine. Still available
in kit form. The first post–WWII civilian aircraft to use a NACA
wing design.

Culver LCA Cadet

Length: 17'8" (5.3 m)   *Wingspan:* 26'11" (8.1 m)   *Cruising speed:*
120 mph (193 km/h)

Rare. A *very small low-wing retractable;* dihedral in wings, none
in tail plane. Overhead, there is a *semi-elliptical curve to both edges
of wings and tail plane.* Plane has a distinct sculptured look to it,
with smooth curves everywhere, as though carved from a bar of soap.
Structure mainly wood, with early fiberglass reinforcement and fuselage skin.
Built from 1939 through WWII, with a few bench-built copies as
late as 1960. Final design was by Al Mooney, creator of the Mooney
line of aircraft; the fastest and nimblest of pre–WWII private aircraft.
Used during the war as radio-controlled target drone, and pilot-flown
as "camera-gun" target for training Air Force gunners and pilots. So
acrobatic, it was a satisfactory imitation of the hottest enemy fighter
planes. It is one of the curiosities of life that Al Mooney was never
brought in to design U.S. fighter planes.

Beech T-34A, B Mentor

Length: 25'10" (7.80 m)   *Wingspan:* 32'10" (10 m)   *Cruising speed:*
160 mph (257 km/h)

Not common. Large *greenhouse canopy* over tandem dual-control
cockpit; *large, slablike, upright tail fin.* The clear "trainer look" combined with a nonradial engine separates the Mentor from the Texan
and the Trojan.
In civilian hands, a popular low-wing aerobatic aircraft. In military
service from 1954 to 1960 as a common USAF and Navy basic
trainer, replacing the T-6 Trojan. Flown by the Navy only from 1960
to 1980. The Air Force moved to all-through jet training during the
years from 1960 to 1964, when most of the civilian-owned Mentors
came on the market. Curiously, after all-through jet training was
deemed a failure by the Air Force, it turned to Cessna's 172 Skyhawk
(page 78), a slow, high-wing prop plane, for the first 30 hours of
training, designating it the T-41 Mescalero.

46

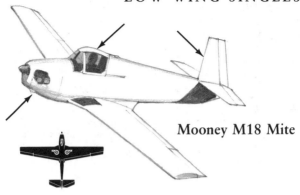

Mooney M18 Mite

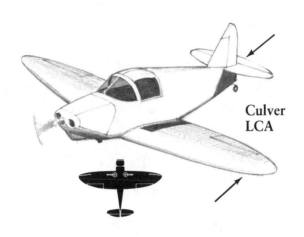

Culver
LCA

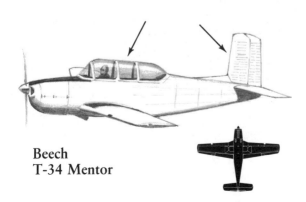

Beech
T-34 Mentor

North American T-6 Texan, Harvard II

Length: 29'6" (8.99 m)   *Wingspan:* 42' (12.80 m)   *Cruising speed:* 218 mph (351 km/h)

A fairly common relic of WWII. *Long greenhouse canopy* over tandem dual controls; *dihedral in wing begins a few feet out from fuselage* (a "reverse gull-wing," as in Corsair). Close at hand or overhead, note the *rounded bump where the leading edge of the wing meets the fuselage;* this is a fairing to hold the retracted main gear wheels. *Tail fin is quite triangular.*

Built before 1941 and in service through the Korean conflict, the Texan, purchased as military surplus, was a popular sport plane for veteran pilots. More often seen parked than in the air. Attention-attracting noise, when flying. More than 15,000 produced between 1941 and 1951. Overhead, the wing is typical of pre–WWII design: nearly straight trailing edge, tapering leading edge — like a single-engine DC3.

North American T-28 Trojan

Length: 32' (9.76 m)   *Wingspan:* 40'1" (12.23 m)   *Cruising speed:* 190 mph (306 km/h)

Not common. In civilian colors; *fat engine cowling* houses large radial engine; *long, high, Plexiglas canopy* sits atop tandem-seating dual controls; *tall, sharply angular tail fin. Plane is heavy, chunky.*

In the 1950s and 1960s, the common U.S. armed forces basic trainer. Sank like a rock with engine failure. It was adapted, like many trainers, to a counterinsurgency role with underwing bomb and rocket mounts. A counterinsurgency role usually implies enough power to carry bombs, but only against a lightly defended target. There have been a few civilian conversions with cabins replacing the cockpit/canopy, but the general configuration is unchanged.

Grumman TBF-1 (TBM-1) Avenger, "Borate Bomber"

Length: 40' (12.2 m)   *Wingspan:* 54'2" (16.5 m)   *Cruising speed:* 240 mph (386 km/h)

A *very rare, large, single-engine* military aircraft. *Original greenhouse cockpit canopy usually modified, but not in any standard manner; lower fuselage (bomb bay) steps up to tail section; square-cut tail surfaces.*

Now restricted to museums and air shows, except for a few that are flying, particularly in Canada, as aerial forest-fire fighters, dropping "borated" or otherwise treated water on fires. Gawky, ungainly, but a fairly successful torpedo bomber. Held a crew of three: the pilot, bombardier/navigator, and gunner. The TBM-1 was identical, manufactured by General Motors under license from Grumman.

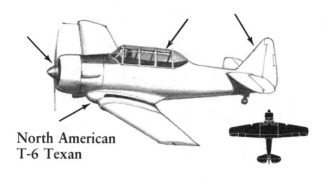

North American
T-6 Texan

North American
T-28 Trojan

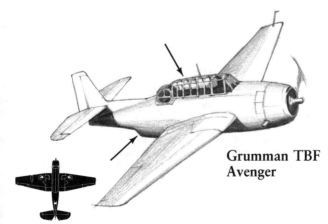

Grumman TBF
Avenger

Chance Vought F-4U Corsair

Length: 33'8" (10.26 m)   *Wingspan:* 41' (12.49 m)   *Cruising speed:* 350 mph (563 km/h)

Unmistakable. *A large, noisy, radial-engine warship* with a one-man cockpit set halfway back on the fuselage. *Wings drop down from fuselage, then show sharp dihedral to tip: "reverse gullwing."* May be seen in hangars with the wings folded up.

More than 12,000 F-4Us were produced through WWII; saw most service in 1944 and 1945. One of the most powerful (2000–3000 horsepower, six .50-caliber machine guns, plus two tons of bombs or rockets) fighter-bombers ever built. Nicknamed "Whistling Death" by Japanese pilots.

North American P-51 Mustang

Length: 32'3" (9.83 m)   *Wingspan:* 37' (11.28 m)   *Cruising speed:* 390 mph (628 km/h)

Rare. Most often seen at air shows. *Long, slim nose with massive propeller spinner.* From the side or below, note that the *radiator air intake* for the liquid-cooled engine is *set well back under the cockpit* (visible in lower sketch). Tail arrangement is unusual; *tail planes set very high and well forward* (to clear the full-length rudder on the tail fin).

Developed by North American in 1940 to meet a British specification for a long-range fighter-escort for British bombers that would operate over Europe from bases in England. Top drawing shows the most common P-51D, with a bubble canopy for good vision to the rear. Bottom sketch shows the turtleback style of the P-51A-C types. The Cavalier Aircraft Company has built modern P-51-Ds with *tip-tanks* to be used as counterinsurgency planes by U.S. allies. This design was acquired by Piper Aircraft, which continued to develop the aircraft as the "Enforcer" until 1984. Counterinsurgency aircraft, as we have noted, are best defined as easily maintained fighter-bombers for use against lightly defended persons and dwellings.

Curtiss P-40 Warhawk, Tomahawk, Kittyhawk

Length: 33'4" (10.05 m)   *Wingspan:* 37'4" (11.3 m)   *Cruising speed:* 315 mph (507 km/h)

Rare, but recently increasing to a few dozen. Compared to other WWII restorations: *Low, rounded tail fin, huge and obvious airscoop under quite pointed propeller spinner, greenhouse canopy.*

Many of the restorations will show the grinning-teeth paint job of the American volunteer Flying Tigers. The P-40, along with the P-39 Cobras, carried the Army Air Force through the first two years of WWII. Ruggedness and reliability were more outstanding than speed or maneuverability; many in Allied air forces; most saw action in the Pacific theater. The final and most numerous production model, P40N, is illustrated.

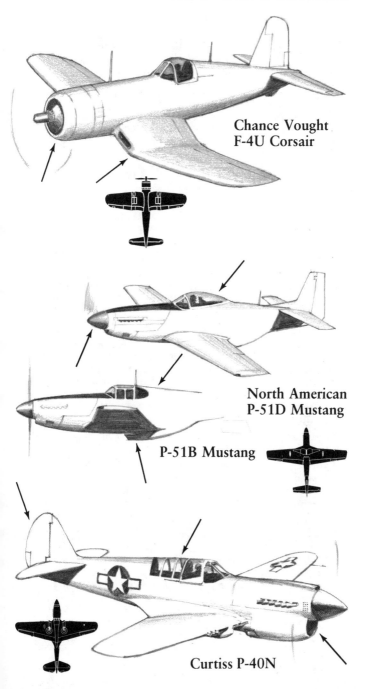

Chance Vought
F-4U Corsair

North American
P-51D Mustang

P-51B Mustang

Curtiss P-40N

de Havilland (Canada) DHC3 Otter

Length: 41'10" (12.80 m)   *Wingspan:* 58' (17.69 m)   *Cruising speed:* 121 mph (195 km/h)

Fairly common in the Far West, Alaska, and Canada. *Massive single-braced high-wing tail-dragger, with huge radial engine;* nearly two-thirds the size of a DC3. If you've never seen a de Havilland Beaver or Otter before, note the passenger windows — Otters show six rectangular side windows behind a cockpit window configuration that's similar to the much smaller Beaver.

Built from 1952 to 1967, this late design carries the most massive, antique appearing tail assembly of any post–WWII aircraft. Essentially an upscaled Beaver (the design project was called "King Beaver"), it carries up to ten passengers. Single 600-horsepower radial engine proved quite reliable, even in the Arctic. Not uncommon on floats, particularly with small Alaskan and Canadian air-taxi operators.

de Havilland (Canada) DHC2 Beaver, U-6

Length: 30'4" (9.24 m)   *Wingspan:* 48' (14.64 m)   *Cruising speed:* with radial, 135 mph (217 km/h); with turboprop, 157 mph (253 km/h)

A common float plane; less common elsewhere. *Massive single-braced high wing,* much more common with radial engine (top drawing). Land versions with *fixed one-rung ladder.* Factory-standard *float planes with multirunged ladder and curved ventral finlet under tail fin. Trapezoidal passenger window with trailing "porthole" window* is typical on all models.

Built from 1948 to 1969; seats up to eight, including the pilot. All-metal construction. Numbers of them have crashed and been totally rebuilt. The less common turboprop (built between 1964 and 1969) also introduced the swept tail fin of modern design, as it did a fuselage-lengthening that put the cabin forward of the wing (bottom sketch).

Noorduyn Norseman, C-64

Length: 32'4" (9.86 m)   *Wingspan:* 51'8" (15.75 m)   *Cruising speed:* 141 mph (227 km/h)

Extremely rare, seen most often in Canada. With its *huge single radial engine,* and typically on floats or skis, it could be confused with a de Havilland, but note the odd *bent landing gear,* which always shows whether above wheels or floats or skis; *rounded wing and tail plane tips; odd geometry and layout of windows; deep fuselage* usually reveals its structure, *fabric over metal tubing.*

Built in various models from 1937 to 1950, over 700 in U.S. armed forces during WWII (USAF C-64, USN JA-1). It was a premier short-haul airliner just after the war, and survives in limited numbers throughout the northern woods and lakes. Carried ten in military discomfort (bucket seats) and six in upholstered airliner seating.

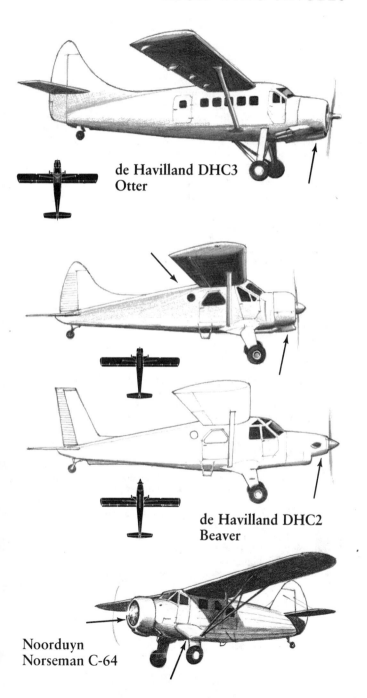

de Havilland DHC3
Otter

de Havilland DHC2
Beaver

Noorduyn
Norseman C-64

Cessna 190/195 Businessliner

Length: 27′1″ (8.26 m)   *Wingspan:* 36′2″ (11 m)   *Cruising speed:* 160 mph (257 km/h)

Rare. A unique combination of *a tail-dragger with skinny spring-steel wheel struts; big radial engine in a bumpy cowling; all-metal skin; and unbraced high wing.* Nothing else puts all that together.

A four-place luxury plane built from 1947 to 1954, the largest, fastest, roomiest, and easily the most expensive of the early postwar private planes. Model numbers refer to type of engine. A factory-standard float plane incorporated a three-finned tail, instead of the usual single tail fin, for lateral stability to overcome the wind drift on the floats — a tail like a miniature version of the Lockheed Constellation.

Howard DGA15, Nightingale

Length: 24′10″ (7.57 m)   *Wingspan:* 38′ (11.58 m) *Cruising speed:* 180 mph (290 km/h)

Very rare. Everything about this plane is heavy, oversized: *Large radial in smooth cowling; big propeller spinner; heavy gear, always with wheel pants; fixed two-rung ladder; tall tail fin;* nearby, the *V-struts enter a distinct underwing fairing.*

Developed from a long-distance racer design, the D(amn) G(ood) A(irplane) 15 was produced from 1939 (50 civilian versions) to 1942 (500 military models). Exceptionally roomy, it was a flying ambulance for the Navy (Nightingale) and a multipurpose trainer. High-powered, not easy to fly, not particularly forgiving. Its printable nickname was "Ensign Eliminator."

Curtiss—Wright Robin

Length: 24′ (7.31 m)   *Wingspan:* 41′ (12.5 m)   *Cruising speed:* 85 mph (137 km/h)

One of the rarest high-wing planes illustrated. *Enormous wing,* not only long, but with a 6-foot constant chord. Curious *wing braces are parallel with several auxiliary struts. Big wheels* on the main gear; *squared-off trailing edge to tail fin* is unusual in such an antique aircraft.

Douglas "Wrong-Way" Corrigan, who had worked on Charles Lindbergh's *Spirit of St. Louis,* made the Curtiss—Wright Robin forever immortal (accounting for the large interest in restoring and re-creating the 1928–1930 aircraft) by "accidentally" flying one from Long Island, New York, to Ireland in 1938 — he always maintained that he was trying to fly nonstop to Los Angeles, but his compass reversed and he flew 180 degrees off course. Built to seat three: the pilot followed by a pair of wicker seats that could be offset to keep shoulders from rubbing. Corrigan flew his from a rear seat, peering over an auxiliary gas tank in the front seat.

Cessna Businessliner

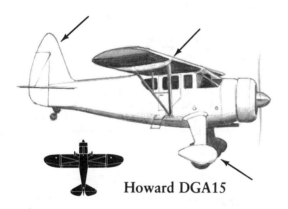

Howard DGA15

Curtiss–Wright Robin

Stinson Reliant, AT-19 (V77)

Length: 27'10" (8.48 m)   *Wingspan:* 41'11" (12.77 m)   *Cruising speed:* 120 mph (193 km/h)

Uncommon. A *massive braced high-wing, always with cowled radial engine.* Typical wing has a single strut; earliest models a pair of almost parallel struts. *Unique wing shape: swollen over strut area, gives the illusion of a gull-wing.* Earliest models also have a "corrugated" cowling; typical surplus AT-19s and all late models have a smooth cowling.

The gull-wing Stinson Reliants appeared in 1935, continuing until 1942 as the lend-lease trainer and transport designated AT-19, used for radio and radar training in Great Britain. One of the earliest four- to five-seaters, it was not an uncommon short-haul airliner and company executive plane. A few battered models still flying as bush planes.

Monocoupe 90

Length: 20'6" (6.25 m)   *Wingspan:* 32' (9.75 m)   *Cruising speed:* 115 mph (185 km/h)

Quite rare. Something about this *V-braced, high-winged, radial-engined* aircraft catches the eye. It is extremely short, but *wide-cabined, with very narrow rear fuselage; cowling bumps over cylinder heads; very small propeller spinner.*

Designed in Moline, Illinois, in the golden age of amateur enthusiasm. Built from 1930 to 1942. Extremely agile little plane, used successfully in aerobatic and closed-course racing during the 1930s. Once the most popular high-performance small plane, it sat two in side-by-side comfort. Charles A. Lindbergh, who could fly anything he wanted, owned a Monocoupe.

Fairchild 24, UC-61 Forwarder (Argus)

Length: 23'9" (7.23 m)   *Wingspan:* 36'4" (11.07 m)   *Cruising speed:* 120 mph (193 km/h)

No longer common. *Roomy, high-backed fuselage* gives the impression of a small airliner; *V-braced high wing has a return strut to the wing root; notch* (for visibility) *in wing over windshield is unique,* so is the landing gear brace: *one wheel brace from fuselage, other from wing brace.*

Built from 1932 to 1947, including several hundred wartime UC-61s. About half the production was with a large radial engine, but most of those still flying are the illustrated in-line types. However, the field marks are consistent. Unusually roomy interiors sat four in military and post–1938 models. The sleek design was influenced by Raymond Loewy, creator of the Coke bottle and the Super Chief train.

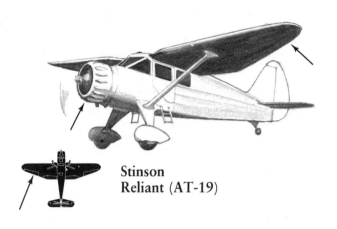

Stinson
Reliant (AT-19)

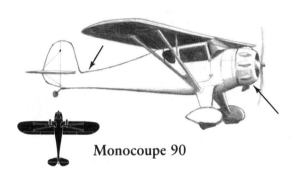

Monocoupe 90

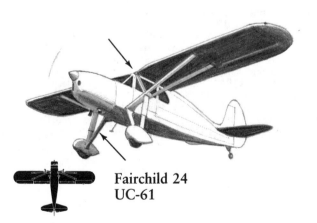

Fairchild 24
UC-61

Rearwin Skyranger

Length: 21'9" (6.6 m)   *Wingspan:* 34' (10.36 m)   *Cruising speed:* 100 mph (161 km/h)

Very rare. This *small, fabric-covered, high-winged tail-dragger* is best singled out by a *disproportionately large tail fin and single side window.*

Never manufactured in large numbers (some 350 between 1940 and 1946), the little Skyranger was a comfortably furnished sport plane that came on the market at the time that most manufacturers were dedicating their efforts to the pre–WWII pilot training programs. Sat two, side by side, with standard dual controls, and, for the time, an unusual "slotted" wing that gave aileron control at exceptionally low speeds. It has a landing speed of 48 mph.

Fleet Canuck

Length: 22'5" (6.83 m)   *Wingspan:* 34' (10.36 m)   *Cruising speed:* 85 mph (137 km/h)

Rare, except in Canada. Not just another *V-braced constant-chord* (width) *high-wing.* A much jauntier look than the similarly sized Piper Cub; more like the very similar Taylorcraft Model B (page 66). Close by, note the *rectangular side window with trailing triangular quarter window.* Compare windows and tail fin shape with Taylorcraft before deciding.

Just over 200 built from 1946 to 1951. A popular light bush plane and a common club and trainer for Canadians — the least expensive plane available and built in Canada to boot. Somewhat overbuilt for strength, it was not certified for aerobatics, but more than one owner has looped it. Hard to stall or spin, with a leisurely landing speed of 44 mph.

Stinson Sentinel, L-5

Length: 24'1" (7.34 m)   *Wingspan:* 34' (10.37 m)   *Cruising speed:* 115 mph (185 km/h)

Rare. One of the few aircraft whose total impression is more distinct than individual field marks. The relatively *massive, sweeping tail,* much like a B-17 tail fin; the *upturned nose;* and the *sweeping belly curve from nose to tail* are distinctive. Close by, note the unique cross-bracing of the side windows, making *three triangular panes.* A very few of these have been converted by civilian owners to normal-looking cockpit canopies.

From 1941 to 1944, 5000 were built. The "Flying Jeep" was the second most common "grasshopper" in the U.S. armed forces, right behind the Piper L-4. Sat two in tandem, but with a hinged rear canopy it served as a flying stretcher-bearer. General George Patton, among others, had an L-5 as a personal aircraft.

**Rearwin
Skyranger**

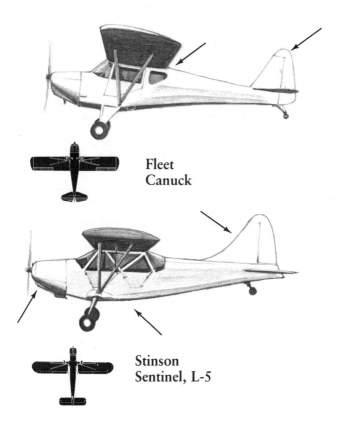

**Fleet
Canuck**

**Stinson
Sentinel, L-5**

Cessna L-19 or O-1 Bird Dog, Ector Mountaineer

Length: 25'10" (7.89 m)   *Wingspan:* 36' (10.9 m)   *Cruising speed:* 105 mph (169 km/h)

Not common. *An uncomplicated little single-brace, high-wing tail-dragger; almost vertical windshield; wraparound rear window; curiously noncongruent side windows; noticeable* (2.8-degree) *wing dihedral.*

More than 3000 Bird Dogs were built from 1950 to 1958, many in civilian use. The Ector Mountaineer was a 1980s revival, built from off-the-shelf or reconditioned parts and more powerful engines. Ector also built the float brackets in as a standard item. Whether Bird Dog or Ector, the odd windows and the all-metal skin make it fairly easy to identify.

Maule, Maule Rocket

Length: 23'7" (7.19 m)   *Wingspan:* 32'11" (10.03 m)   *Cruising speed:* 160 mph (257 km/h)

Although there are several models of Maules with slight external variations, the combination of *rectangular wing with turned-down cambered tips, simple streamlined V-bracing* (no return bracings, no wires), and a *deep but not very tall tail fin* should identify the Rocket. Relatively few older planes have the rounded tail fin shown in the partial sketch. The original wheel fairings (main drawing) are increasingly uncommon. More now on tricycle gear, many on floats or skis. A longer nose, plus twin exhausts, indicates a turboprop.

The other way to identify a Rocket is to watch one take off when the pilot is in the mood to show off: The M-6 Super Rocket needs a roll of only 125 feet (38 m) — that's less than the width of a football field. The difference between maximum speed (150 mph; 241 km/h) and stalling speed (35 mph; 57 km/h) is truly remarkable.

Champion/Bellanca Citabria, Scout, Decathlon

Length: 22'8" (6.91 m)   *Wingspan:* 33'5" (10.19 m)   *Cruising speed:* 125 mph (201 km/h)

Of the small, *V-braced, constant-chord, square-end winged* planes on this page, the Citabria is best distinguished by its *fancy wheel pants* and *squared-off tail fin.*

Champion Aircraft was manufacturing the tail-dragging Champion Traveller before it shifted to this version in 1964, with its more modern tail surfaces and wheel treatment, plus strengthening that made it certifiable as an aerobatic plane (Citabria is Airbatic, backward). One of the first planes capable of continuous inverted flight. From 1970 to 1980, Bellanca also built a nonaerobatic Scout and a strengthened, fully aerobatic Decathlon.

Cessna Bird Dog, L-19

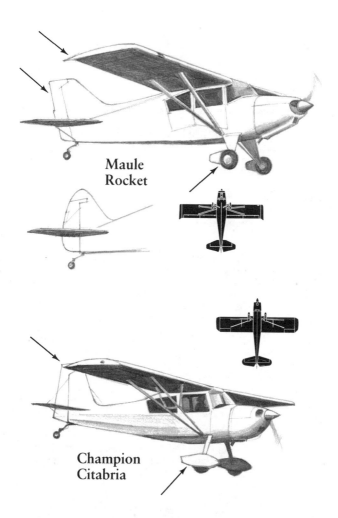

Maule
Rocket

Champion
Citabria

Arctic Tern, Interstate Cadet (L-6)

Length: 24' (7.32 m) *Wingspan:* 36' (10.97 m) *Cruising speed:* 115 mph (185 km/h)

Not common. Another of those darned *constant-chord, V-braced, high-wing tail-draggers.* A tandem-seat, slim plane whose most distinguishing feature is the *tall, pointy tail fin, with noticeable trim-tab showing at tail plane level.* New versions (top drawing) have squared-off wing tips; older Interstates and L-6s have round tips. The *2 degrees of dihedral in the wing* are, as usual, quite noticeable.

Very few of the originals survive, including the L-6 (not illustrated), which was an Interstate Cadet (bottom sketch) with a greenhouse-type cockpit window. Interstate Cadets produced from 1937 to 1942 as trainers; L-6 until 1944. The design was revived in 1969 in Alaska, where the Arctic Tern (top drawing) continues to be bench-built, but with three visible changes: square wing tips, angular rear passenger window, and tail wheel moved all the way to the rear.

Funk (Akron) Model B to Model L

Length: 20' (6.1 m) *Wingspan:* 35' (10.7 m) *Cruising speed:* 100 mph (161 km/h)

Quite rare. One of the two *braced high-wing singles with a pair of parallel braces* (see the Porterfield Collegiate, page 64). Head on, the Funk engine cowling is quite unique, showing *round air intake completely surrounding propeller spinner. Massive tail fin; squat, chunky overall appearance.*

Built from 1939 to WWII and again from 1946 to 1948. A side-by-side two-seater that was considered remarkably easy to fly, responsive, but stable (note the large high-lift wing and the substantial stabilizing tail assembly).

Stinson 10A (Voyager 90), Voyager 108, Voyager 108-1, -2, -3

Length: 22' (6.71 m) *Wingspan:* 34' (10.37 m) *Cruising speed:* 108 mph (174 km/h)

Not common, and not just another braced high-wing tail-dragger. Though the Voyager's general shape is unique, concentrate on some fairly trivial field marks for positive identification. All the Voyagers have a noticeable (2-degree) dihedral in the wing.

Voyager 90, model 10A (top drawing): The two-seat side-by-side, with a possible third bench seat behind the pilot. *The V-brace to the wing* is quite unusual in that it has *no supplementary cross or up-braces* (contrast a typical Piper Cub). *Tail plane is set extremely low.* Although distinctly a fabric-covered plane, the general effect is clean and neat, if stubby. Built from 1939 to 1942, when it was replaced by the military L-5 (page 58).

Voyager 108 (bottom drawing): The four-seat Voyager, built from 1946 to 1948, looks much sleeker and slimmer than the Voyager 90 and has a *longer engine cowling,* housing an engine twice as powerful as the pre-war Voyager's. Same *simple V-brace* without any supplements.

Voyager 108-3 (bottom sketch): The last Voyager, with the *much larger, vertical-style tail.* Seats four. A few of the 108-3s were built by Piper until 1950.

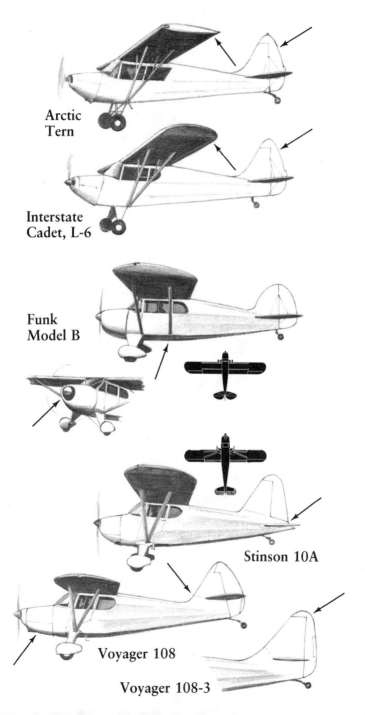

Arctic Tern

Interstate Cadet, L-6

Funk Model B

Stinson 10A

Voyager 108

Voyager 108-3

Porterfield Collegiate

Length: 22'8" (6.9 m)   *Wingspan:* 34'9" (11 m)   *Cruising speed:* 100 mph (161 km/h)

Quite rare. One of two *high-wing singles with parallel double struts.* Compare with Funk (Akron) Model B (above), a much chunkier, squatter aircraft with a larger tail fin. All fabric. If there was nothing left of a Collegiate but the engine cowling, you could identify it by the *distinct cut-in for engine exhaust.*

A tandem-seat trainer and sportster; only about 500 built before WWII put Porterfield out of the airplane business and into manufacturing troop gliders in preparation for the invasion of Europe. As a trainer, extremely popular with students; with hands off, it would recover from spins or stalls and, for the nervous, could land at speeds as low as 40 mph (64 km/h).

Aeronca Champ, Traveller, Tri-Traveller, L-16

Length: 21'6" (6.56 m)   *Wingspan:* 35' (10.66 m)   *Cruising speed:* 90 mph (145 km/h)

Very similar to the Aeronca Tandem, and the Aeronca Chief; separate from the Tandem by the Champ's *smooth engine cowling,* from the Chief by the slimmer fuselage/cabin, indicating its tandem seating.

Built from 1948 to 1964, the last dozen years by the Champion Aircraft Company, which acquired the design from Aeronca. Military observation versions (L-16) had four large, square side windows, otherwise identical. Champion Aircraft called it the Traveller and also manufactured more than 1000 Tri-Travellers, a popular flight instruction model. The Tri-Traveller sits on its tricycle gear with its nose distinctly turned up, quite noticeable on the flight line.

Aeronca Chief, Super Chief

Length: 21' (6.3 m)   *Wingspan:* 36' (10.9 m)   *Cruising speed:* 95 mph (153 km/h)

A pair of somewhat *stubby, braced high-wing two-seaters.* Like so many WWII planes, it's of *fabric construction,* with constant-chord (width) wings and rounded tips. Close at hand, *Aeronca's trailing edge of the tail fin shows a noticeable extrusion* — an adjustable trim-tab. Once you've positively noted this, you'll find the shape of the entire plane sufficiently distinctive for long-range identification. The *Super Chief tail is much larger* (bottom sketch). The *Champion is very similar; its slimmer fuselage indicates the tandem-seating for two.* The original Chief was designed to take Continental's revolutionary opposed four-cylinder engine; first flown in 1938. With side-by-side seating for two, it was cosier than contemporary tandems, including the popular Piper Cubs. The Chief production ended in 1948. The Super Chief was built between 1946 and 1950.

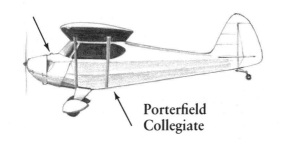

Porterfield
Collegiate

Aeronca
Champ

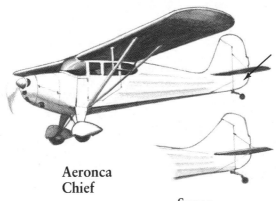

Aeronca
Chief

Super
Chief

Aeronca 15AC Sedan

Length: 25'3" (7.70 m)   *Wingspan:* 37'6" (11.43 m)   *Cruising speed:* 114 mph (183 km/h)

A rare *high-wing tail-dragger:* The *single-wing brace attaches much farther outboard* than somewhat similar Cessna high-wings. The distinctive *tail fin appears to lean forward and shows the typical Aeronca bump.*

Never common, the Sedan (close at hand, note the automobile-style door and window configuration) was built from 1947 to 1950. Perhaps 120 are still flying, some on floats. A roomy four-seater with good "high and hot" flying characteristics, it's capable of taking off with less than 500 feet of ground roll at sea level. Came standard with dual controls.

Taylorcraft Model B, Taylorcraft F19, F21 Sportsman, F-22 Classic

Length: 22'1" (6.73 m)   *Wingspan:* 36' (10.97 m)   *Cruising speed:* 115 mph (185 km/h)

A variety of airplanes, based on a pre–WWII design, but in production as late as 1982. *Large, upright tail fin with a distinct flat spot on the rudder; long, slim fuselage appears to "pinch down" to the tail assembly.* Compare carefully with Taylorcraft Model D and L-2 Grasshopper (next drawing). Lowest-priced Model Bs lacked the rear quarter-window. F-22 has tricycle gear.

The classic Model B Taylorcrafts, built from 1938 to 1958, lacked such niceties as wheel pants; so did the Taylorcraft F19 Sportsman, built by the revived company in 1968 (top drawing). Most sat two side by side, but a few were built in the 1950s to seat four. The revived Taylorcraft F19 and the wheel-panted (or, as they say in Britain, the "spatted-wheel") F21 returned to the two-seater format.

Taylorcraft Model D, L-2, O-57

Length: 22'1" (6.73 m)   *Wingspan:* 36' (10.97 m)   *Cruising speed:* 90 mph (145 km/h)

Fairly common. Compare closely to the Taylorcraft Model B, noting that it has the same large tail with a flat spot on the rudder. Always with *exposed cylinder heads* (but so were a few Model Bs). If tandem seating is visible, that separates it from the Model Bs; so does the A-shaped supplementary brace from the V-brace to the wing (Model B and F19 and F21 have a rectangular supplementary brace).

The L-2, with *greenhouse canopy and cut-down fuselage* (bottom sketch), was a popular war-surplus purchase.

There was no advantage to retooling from the dual control Model B trainers to the Model D Tandem trainer, except that it was the general wisdom that instructors should ride behind, not next to, the student. Several thousand Tandems and L-2s (also known as O-57) were built from 1941 to 1945.

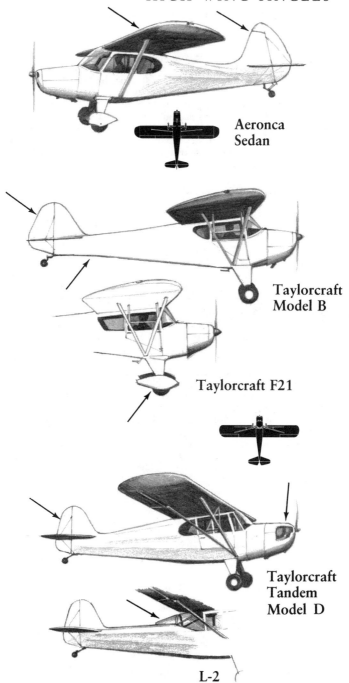

HIGH-WING SINGLES

Aeronca
Sedan

Taylorcraft
Model B

Taylorcraft F21

Taylorcraft
Tandem
Model D

L-2

Aeronca Tandem 65T, L-3

Length: 22'4" (6.8 m)   *Wingspan:* 35' (10.6 m)   *Cruising speed:* 80 mph (130 km/h)

Not common. Shares some field marks with early Piper Cubs. *Engine cylinders show through cowling* (as on Piper J3) but Tandem's cowling looks pug-nosed. A small *triangular brace was added to main wing braces. Tail rounded* (note flat spot on Piper J3 Cub tail). The rear window shape is unique.

The Tandem was designed in 1940 for the pre–WWII Civilian Pilot Training Program — it's basically an Aeronca Chief with tandem seating. The rear seat, in a useful invention, was suspended six inches higher than the front seat for visibility. The Army Air Force ordered thousands of Tandems with extra windows (bottom sketch) as the L-3, a liaison and observation airplane.

Piper J3 Cub Trainer, PA11 Cub Special, J5 Cub Cruiser, PA12 Super Cruiser, J4 Cub Coupe, L-4

Length: 22'4" (6.80 m)   *Wingspan:* 35'3" (10.74 m)   *Cruising speeds:* J3, 80 mph; Super Cruiser, 100 mph (129–161 km/h)

Not every *constant-chord* (width) *high-wing, fabric tail-dragger* is a Cub; it just seems that way.

J3 (top drawing): *Exposed cylinder heads* (compare Aeronca Tandem, L-3), *V-brace, and distinct flat spot on tail.* Some 5000 built before WWII. A popular tandem-seat, two-man trainer that introduced nearly 75 percent of WWII aviators to flying, mostly through the Civilian Pilot Training program. More than 5000 built for WWII observation-liaison as L-4.

PA11 Cub Special, J5 Cub Cruiser, PA12 Super Cruiser (middle sketch): In spite of a variety of engines and names, these are all *three-seaters* (one pilot seat, and two passenger seats to the rear), with *fully enclosed engine.* Several hundred still flying, particularly the higher-powered Super Cruisers; many on floats. About 6000 built of the various three-seaters.

J4 Cub Coupe (bottom drawing): Rarest of all. Compare closely to Super Cub (next entry) before deciding. *Engine cowling shows a distinct bump over cylinder heads* (compare middle sketch and Super Cub drawing), *a pudgy, dumpy look* caused by stuffing a side-by-side two-person cockpit onto the slim J3 Cub fuselage, which was designed for tandem seating. The J4 Cub Coupe tail is more rounded than the J3, etc., making it quite similar to Super Cub tail.

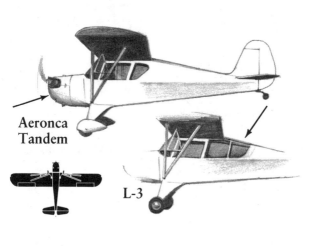

Aeronca
Tandem

L-3

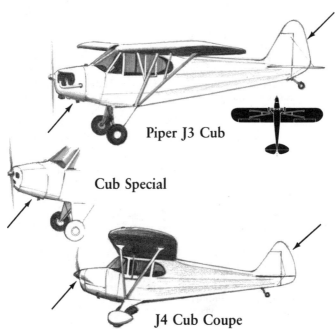

Piper J3 Cub

Cub Special

J4 Cub Coupe

Piper PA18 Super Cub, L-18

Length: 22'7" (6.88 m)   *Wingspan:* 35'2" (10.73 m)   *Cruising speed:* 115 mph (185 km/h)

Common as crabgrass. *Tail-dragging, all-fabric, rounded-tip, constant-chord* (width), *braced high-wing,* with *smooth cowling completely enclosing engine.* Compare the J3 and Cub Cruiser (previous entry). *Always something showing below propeller spinner* — a location Piper has used for a variety of engine air intakes, landing lights, etc., all absent on the earlier Cubs.

First flown in 1949, kept in production (from inventory parts) as late as 1982, although dropped from Piper's official list that year. The success of the tandem two-seat Super Cub with standard dual controls was unquestioned — more than 30,000 were sold in the first 22 years of production. While the Super Cub endured, the various three- and four-seat Cubs were dropped in favor of new low-wing designs. The Super Cub, with more sophisticated construction methods (metal instead of wood wing spars, for example), is still essentially a power upgrade of the old tandem, two-seat J3.

Aviat Christen Husky A-1

Length: 22'7" (6.88 m)   *Wingspan:* 35'2" (10.73 m)   *Cruising speed:* 140 mph (226 km/h)

Superficially, it looks as if someone dinged a Supercub and replaced the wing with a Maule part. But note the *wide rectangular wing* combined with a more *old-fashioned-looking tail plane. Rectangular side windows.*

Christen took over the old Pitts factory (see both their sporting biplanes earlier in the book) in Wyoming and designed this brand-new utility airplane from scratch. Now a division of AVIAT. The only cloth-over-tubing factory monoplane built today. The U.S. Border Patrol is replacing its Supercubs with Huskies. Increasingly common on floats, or with superwide tundra tires.

Luscombe 8A-8F, Silvaire

Length: 20' (6.09 m)   *Wingspan:* 35' (10.66 m)   *Cruising speed:* 105 mph (169 km/h)

Uncommon. A *small all-metal* plane, usually finished in *plain polished aluminum.* Strong men refer to it as "dainty" and "beautiful." Pre-war models had fabric-covered wings. Wings show slight tapers toward the tip, separating it quickly from its constant-chord cohort. A distinct notch in the trailing edge of the wing over the cockpit is visible; it's similar to biplane upper wings. Compare the Cessna 140 before being sure.

A pure sport and touring two-seater, designed in 1937 by Don Luscombe, author of the Monocoupe light plane design. Only 1200 built before WWII, but more than 5000 built from 1945 to 1949 by Luscombe. A few more built by Temco, and some bench-built by Silvaire as recently as 1960. Drawing shows the original 8A to 8D models with V-strut; 8E onward had a single strut.

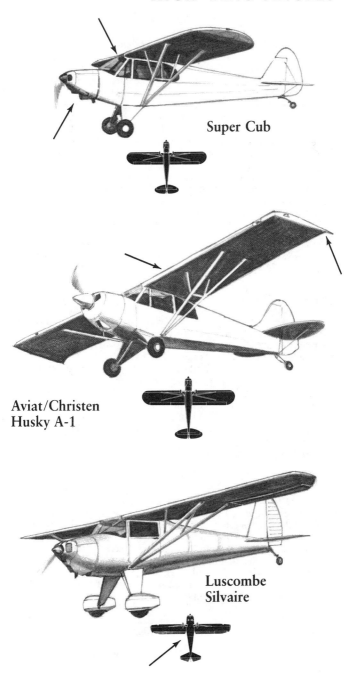

Super Cub

Aviat/Christen
Husky A-1

Luscombe
Silvaire

Cessna 120, 140

Length: 21'6" (6.58 m)   *Wingspan:* 32'10" (10 m)   *Cruising speed:* 105 mph (169 km/h)

Still common. A *braced high-wing, tail-dragging single. Most with two braces on a constant-chord* (width) *wing with rounded tip. Deeply recurved tail planes, rounded tail fin.* The model 120 was a stripped-down version, but the only visible difference is that the *120 lacks the quarter-window behind passenger window.* In 1949–1950, the 140D had the new all-metal Cessna wing and a single-brace — it looks exactly like the model 170 (lower drawing), but with a smaller quarter-window behind the door, and no dorsal fin fairing to the tail fin.

Introduced in 1946, the two-seat Cessna 120/140 was one of the least expensive and highest-powered (85 hp) private airplanes you could buy. The spraddling spring-steel landing gear was so bouncy that the plane was actually more comfortable on grass strips than paved runways, and it matched up nicely with the pasture pilots and small grass airports that were typical of the late 1940s. Nearly 5000 built by 1950, when production ended.

Cessna 170

Length: 25' (7.62 m)   *Wingspan:* 36' (10.96 m)   *Cruising speed:* 110 mph (177 km/h)

Still common. An *all-metal, tail-dragging, braced high-wing single with spring-steel landing gear. The rounded tail fin merging into a long dorsal fin is unique* (other planes with the dorsal fin leading into the tail have more angular tail fins). A few (less than 10 percent) are early models with constant-chord wing and two wing struts, and without the dorsal fin: They resemble the 120/140 (previous entry) but are larger overall, with a much larger rear quarter-window.

The 170 was essentially a trade-up to four seats from the extremely popular Cessna 140. After one year (1948) the company introduced the all-metal tapered wing and subsequently sold nearly 5000 170s. It became the Cessna 172 after eight years of production by the simple addition of a tricycle gear and an angular, less romantic tail fin. Some 170s, meant for paved-only use, have wheel pants on the main gear.

Piper PA20 Pacer, PA22 Tri-Pacer, PA15 Vagabond

Length: 20'4" (6.2 m)   *Wingspan:* 29'4" (8.9 m)   *Cruising speed:* 130 mph (209 km/h)

A set of *braced high-wing singles* with *two struts to wing* (compare similar Cessnas, with a single brace). *Wings similar in shape, but much stubbier than on the Piper Cub and Super Cub.* The Tri-Pacer (top drawing) also shows a large air scoop over the nose gear.

Piper, which had been building the very successful tandem-seat Cub series, decided to add another low-cost item in 1948 and 1949, the fabric-winged PA15 Vagabonds, side-by-side two-seaters. These quickly grew into the four-seat Pacers, with more powerful engines than the Cubs. The much stubbier Pacer wing (about three-quarters the total area of the Cub wing) did allow the Pacer to fly about 20 mph faster than the comparable Cub. Because of the lack of lift in the shorter wing, it climbed about two-thirds as fast as the Cub.

HIGH-WING SINGLES

Cessna 140

Cessna 170

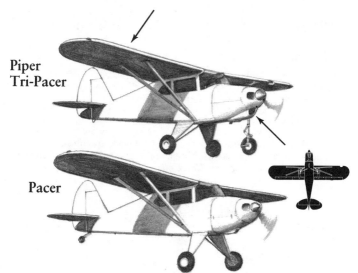

Piper
Tri-Pacer

Pacer

Cessna 180/185 Skywagon, Carryall, Agwagon

Length: 25'9" (7.85 m)   *Wingspan:* 35'10" (10.92 m)   *Cruising speed:* 129 mph (208 km/h)

A *large tail-dragger,* with *braced high wing.* Size, and the presence of three side windows, separates it from the 140/170 (page 72). Has a substantial tail — slightly smaller on the model 180 than on the 185 — but this is difficult to determine the first time, unless the planes are side by side. After you've seen them both, it's quite noticeable.

Produced for 30 years with minor changes (windows, engines, and making the drooping wing tip standard on recent models) since 1953. The big-tailed, six-seat 185, first produced in 1961, is a very common float plane in the north woods. There are standard spray-boom-equipped models for agricultural use; these show not only the booms, but a 160-gallon spray tank that attaches to the fuselage under the cockpit. The slight (less than 2-degree) dihedral in the wing is quite noticeable.

Helio Courier, U-10

Length: 31' (9.45 m)   *Wingspan:* 39' (11.89 m)   *Cruising speed:* 150 mph (241 km/h)

Not common. *Unbraced high, constant-chord* (width) *wing;* usually a tail-dragger; a very few with fixed tricycle gear. On tail-draggers, the *forward gear is on extremely long struts and is set well forward of the wing. Very tall, upright tail fin.*

Manufactured from 1955 to 1978, about half the small production went to the U.S. Air Force as U-10s, a common liaison, cargo, and anti-insurgency plane in the Vietnam War. The only airplane completely designed by Harvard and Massachusetts Institute of Technology faculty members. Full-length leading-edge slotted flaps and massive slotted trailing-edge flaps give it a bizarre short takeoff and landing capability. Seats up to six. Whatever the gear or engine type, the tail and wing configurations are consistent.

Pilatus PC-6 Turbo Porter, UV 20A Chiricahua

Length: 36'1" (11 m)   *Wingspan:* 52'1" (15.87 m)   *Cruising speed:* 132 mph (213 km/h)

The most *rectangular plane* in the air. *Hershey-bar wings and tail planes; fuselage cross section is also rectangular; curious arched windows in passenger door and very long nose.*

Modern, high-performance STOL aircraft. A few early Turbo Porters had a shorter nose than the PC-6, but they still don't look like a turboprop de Havilland Beaver (page 52). A very few with radials still flying. When with landing gear, the wheels are unusually large and on spidery, high struts. Movie fans may remember it as the bad guys' float plane in *Never Cry Wolf.*

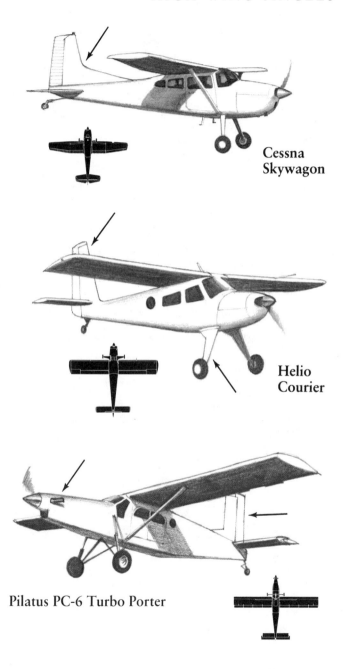

Cessna
Skywagon

Helio
Courier

Pilatus PC-6 Turbo Porter

Cessna 150, 152

Length: 24'1" (7.34 m)   *Wingspan:* 33'2" (10.11 m)   *Cruising speed:* 120 mph (193 km/h)

A series of *small braced high-wing* planes; all two-seaters; commonly fitted with dual controls for training. From 1970 onward, an optional version (the Aerobat) had structural strengthening for aerobatic flying — these will have a pair of cockpit ceiling through-the-wing windows. Some 30,000 150s and 152s were built (most of them resembling the top drawing). Many converted to tail-draggers.

Model 150A, B, C (bottom drawing): Note *two side windows* and *upright tail fin*. About 3000 built from 1959 to 1963.

Model 150D (not illustrated): Built only in 1964; has the single side window and wraparound rear window of the late Model 150s and all Model 152s (top drawing) but with the upright tail fin of the earlier 150s.

Model 150s built from 1965 to 1977, and all Model 152s built after 1977 (top drawing): *Single side window, wraparound rear window, swept tail fin.* The 1965 150Es had a shorter dorsal fin fairing into the swept tail.

North American Rockwell Darter Commander, Lark Commander

Length: Lark, 27'2" (8.28 m)   *Wingspan:* 35' (10.67 m)   *Cruising speed:* 130 mph (209 km/h)

Rare. *Constant-chord wings, with square tips, tricycle gear.* Darter Commander (upper sketch) is 5 feet shorter and has *upright angular tail fin.* Lark Commander (main drawing) stretched the fuselage and added *swept tail fin.*

Odd little four-seaters: designed by the Volaire company, which was acquired by Aero Commander, which was acquired by Rockwell. From 1968 to 1971, Rockwell built fewer than 2000, as the parent company switched to low-wing designs in single-engine aircraft (the Aero Commander 112). Intended to compete with the Cessna 150, of which more than 10,000 had been delivered before the Darter/Lark came on the market.

Cessna 152

Cessna 150

Aero Darter
Commander

Aero Commander
Lark Commander

Cessna 172, 172 Skyhawk, T-41 Mescalero, 175 Skylark, Cutlass, Cutlass RG, Hawk XP

Length: 27'2" (8.28 m)   *Wingspan:* 36'1" (11 m)
Cruising speed: 172 Skyhawk, 140 mph (225 km/h)

Ubiquitous. A series of classic high-wing single Cessnas produced for 30 years. We'll take them in order, from the 1956 introduction of the Cessna 172, essentially a 170 with tricycle landing gear:

Cessna 172 (top drawing): *Two side windows; no rear window; high, unswept tail fin, with corrugated rudder. Squared-off nose* (compare with the 182/Skylane cowling, small sketch above 172 drawing).

Cessna 172 Skyhawk (model years 1960 to 1963) and 1958 model year Skylark (lower drawing): This is the old 172 cabin configuration with *swept tail fin* and *wheel pants.*

Cessna 175 Skylark (1959 to 1962): The Skylark was distinguished, until maintenance problems killed the idea, by a geared down propeller. Note the *hump behind the propeller spinner;* otherwise identical to contemporary Skyhawks.

Cessna 172 Skyhawk (after 1964): Drawing shows the latest model, with a *long dorsal fin fairing to tail fin, and wraparound rear window.* The dorsal fin was shorter when the plane was introduced; it reached this length in 1971. Distinguish it from same-age 182 Skylanes, which have a flat rear window. Skylanes are also bulkier and huskier than Skyhawks, but you should make the distinction close at hand, and then learn the conformation. Some 172s seen in blue and white paint, with "U.S. Air Force" lettered on the side, but without other insignia, in civilian-operated contract flight schools near Air Force training bases, where it is the 30-hour primary trainer, designated T-41 Mescalero.

Cessna Hawk XP (extra performance) (after 1978): A 172 Skyhawk with fixed gear, a more powerful engine, and subtle differences in only the nose cowling. Note the *larger spinner* and the *sleek cowling, with landing lights just above the nose wheel.*

Cessna 172 Cutlass: A 180-horsepower version of the 172 Skyhawk; no visible differences.

Cessna 172 Cutlass RG: *A retractable-gear Skyhawk; wheel wells remain open.* Distinguish from the very similar, but bulkier, retractable Skylane RG by the wraparound rear windshield. After you've seen them both close at hand, the difference in their shape will be a better field mark.

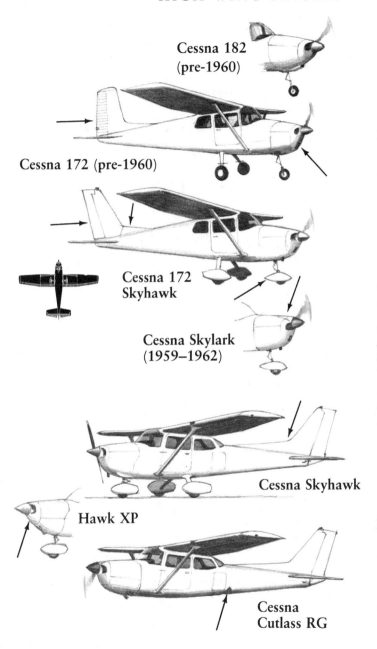

HIGH-WING SINGLES

Cessna 182
(pre-1960)

Cessna 172 (pre-1960)

Cessna 172
Skyhawk

Cessna Skylark
(1959–1962)

Cessna Skyhawk

Hawk XP

Cessna
Cutlass RG

Cessna 182 Skylane, Skylane RG

Length: 28'2" (8.59 m)   *Wingspan:* 35'10" (10.92 m)   *Cruising speed:* 157 mph (253 km/h)

A pair of identical braced high-wing singles. One, the *RG, has retractable gear* (top drawing), which increases the cruising speed to 179 mph (289 km/h). When retracted, note the open wheel wells on each side of the fuselage. Skylanes have a *flat, non-wraparound rear window.* Compare the Cessna 172 series (page 78): Early 172s lacked rear window; later types have wraparound rear window.

What we have here is a more powerful version of the older model 172. But Cessna already had that in the model 180; page 74.

Cessna Stationair, Skywagon, and Super Skylane

Stationair 7 specifications: *Length:* 31'9" (9.68 m)   *Wingspan:* 35'10" (10.92 m)   *Cruising speed:* 156 mph (251 km/h)

Common, variable. A series of pilot plus five- or six-passenger aircraft most easily distinguished from their Cessna stablemates by sheer size; *all with single brace, wheel pants, and swept tail fins.*

Cessna 205 and 206 (Stationair 5, 6) and Super Skylane (top drawing): *three passenger windows.* The more comfortably appointed Super Skylane looks just like a Stationair 6 from the port side but has a single door, not the double cargo doors of a Stationair, on the starboard side. This group has the same wing, but a fuselage length of 28 feet (8.53 m).

Cessna 207, 208 (Stationair 7, 8): Noticeably longer, emphasized by the *four, not three, side windows.*

Until the invention of the fourteen-passenger Caravan, the Stationair 8 was the largest braced-wing Cessna, and one of the larger single-engine planes, made. It will come as no comfort to those who try to put the proper names on things to learn that the original model 206 was called a Skywagon, that the next version, the model 207, was also given that name, and that the 206 was then called a Stationair again. When the final version of the 207 came out, it was called a Stationair 8. Several thousand of all types have been built since 1964. For the real Skywagon, see page 74.

Cessna 208 Caravan

Length: 37'7" (11.46 m)   *Wingspan:* 51'8" (15.75 m)   *Cruising speed:* 214 mph (344 km/h)

New in 1984. A *monster single,* comparable to the de Havilland Otter in size; *single Cessna-style brace to wing; five passenger windows; angular tail surfaces.*

The Caravan, with a single turbocharged 600-horsepower engine, carrying up to 14 people, is an attempt to find a replacement for the no-longer-manufactured de Havilland Otters and Beavers and the many Cessna 180s and 185s. The tall fixed gear is meant for unimproved airstrips. Sales to military services are expected, as ambulance, parachute, and light transport. It can carry a ton and a half of freight more than 1000 miles.

Cessna
Skylane RG

Cessna 182
Skylane

Cessna
Stationair 6

Cessna
Stationair 7, 8

Cessna
Caravan

Cessna 210 Centurion, Turbo Centurion

Length: 28'2" (8.59 m)   *Wingspan:* 36'9" (11.20 m)   *Cruising speed:* Centurion, 193 mph (311 km/h); Turbo, 222 mph (357 km/h)

An *unbraced high-wing.* The *tail plane is mounted slightly higher than on Cardinal series; two large side windows on Centurion, four small windows on pressurized Turbo Centurion* (but compared to Cardinal RG, next drawing). Almost all Centurions have *a dorsal fin that begins at the rear of the cabin* (compare shorter fin on Cardinal RG).

Seating the pilot plus six, the Centurions first flew in 1967. Their combination of unbraced high wing and retractable gear, along with the Cardinal RG, is unique in the industry. The pressurized Centurion was added to the line in 1977. There are a few early models around, built from 1964 to 1966, which have a braced wing, that are virtually indistinguishable from a Cessna Cutlass RG (previous entry). If you see an unbraced-wing Centurion that appears to have a smaller dorsal fin than illustrated (or happen to see a pair of them parked side by side), it is one of the models built in 1967 or 1968. Centurions built from 1969 to 1978 had doors to cover the main landing gear. Models built from 1979 to date have eliminated the doors and show a distinct notch just under the rear of the cabin (typical as on lower drawing of the T210 pressurized Centurion).

Cessna Cardinal Classic, Cardinal RG

Length: 27'3" (8.31 m)   *Wingspan:* 35'6" (10.82 m)   *Cruising speed:* RG, 139 mph (224 km/h)

Anything with an *unbraced wing and fixed tricycle gear is a Cardinal.* The retractable model is best distinguished from the similar Cessna Centurion by *smaller size; dorsal fin to tail begins well behind cabin* on both models; *tail plane set very low* (appears to be glued on, not inserted, as on the Centurion).

More than 4000 of these dapper little planes were built from 1967 until production ceased in 1978. (Early models were designated 177; the name "Cardinal" originally indicated a 177 with more horsepower, fancier interiors, and full blind-flying instrumentation.) The unbraced wing looks attractive, but it actually added little speed, or efficiency. Cessna found that in the four-seater business it was competing with itself, the braced-wing Cessna Skylane RG being a perfectly acceptable, slightly less expensive alternative to the Cardinal RG. The model 177 was withdrawn in 1976, followed by two years of producing only Cardinals.

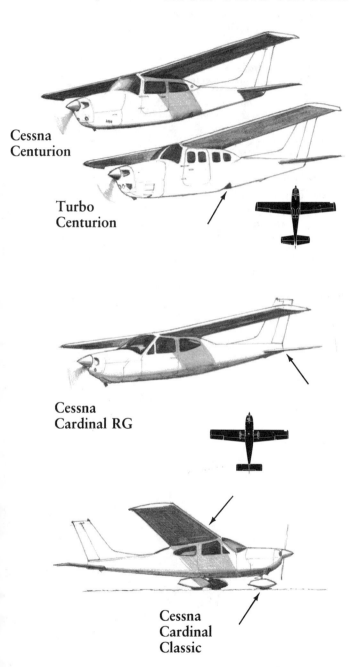

Cessna
Centurion

Turbo
Centurion

Cessna
Cardinal RG

Cessna
Cardinal
Classic

Lake LA-4 Buccaneer, Renegade, Skimmer

Buccaneer specifications: *Length:* 24'11" (7.6 m)   *Wingspan:* 38'
(11.6 m)   *Cruising speed:* 150 mph (241 km/h)

A series of four- to six-place amphibians. High-winged flying boat
or amphibian with a *single engine mounted on a pylon high above
the cabin; pusher propeller.*

Oldest version, Skimmer (center sketch), was a pure flying boat
and lacked the support struts on the engine pylon. Buccaneer (top
drawing), is most common, and is quickly distinguished from the
Renegade by the lower position of the horizontal stabilizer/tail plane.
The Renegade's tail fin control surface is all *below* the tail plane. Recent Lake Renegades (bottom sketch) carry five passengers, and are
four feet (1.22 m) longer than Buccaneers.

TSC1 Teal

Typical Teal II specifications: *Length:* 23'7" (7.19 m)   *Wingspan:*
31'11" (9.73 m)   *Cruising speed:* 115 mph (185 km/h)

Very rare. Most flying are home-builts, but all are easily identifiable: *The only single-engined amphibian with a traction, pulling engine.* T-tail is also unique.

Original Teals came from the factory with standard dual controls,
but most home-builts are single control with seating for three passengers. The original design had fold-up seats, on the presumption that
the average user would be a fisherman who could turn his airplane
into a john boat and fish right from the craft. Sold in kit form in the
1980s.

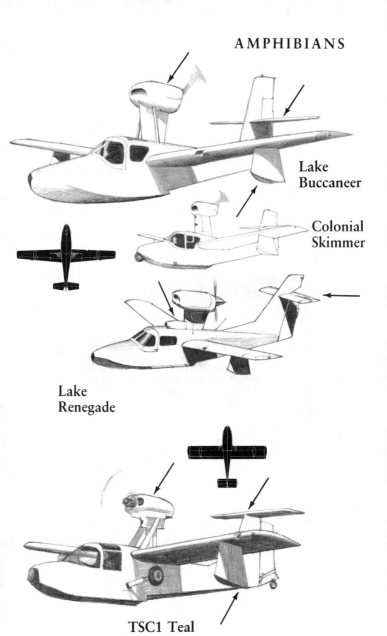

AMPHIBIANS

Lake
Buccaneer

Colonial
Skimmer

Lake
Renegade

TSC1 Teal

Republic RC3 Seabee

Length: 28' (8.53 m)   *Wingspan:* 37'8" (11.48 m)   *Cruising speed:* 105 mph (169 km/h)

A fat-cabined, thin-fuselaged amphibian with a *gently curved leading edge* to the tail fin. *Pusher propeller* mounted on the rear of the cabin.

The Seagull on land is clearly a tail-dragger, and the rear wheel stays down in flight as the two front wheels retract up to, but not into, the fuselage. It was with visions of a vast postwar leisure-time market that the Republic Aviation Company purchased Percy Spencer's design for his home-built Spencer S-12 in 1943 and certified the plane in 1946. It was an era when men were seriously designing flying automobiles as well. Republic cranked out 1080 of the planes in a little more than two years, at a net loss of some $14 million. The mass market never caught up with the costs of tooling up and producing aircraft that sold for less than $6000.

Grumman G21 Goose

Original specifications: *Length:* 38'4" (11.68 m)   *Wingspan:* 49' (14.94 m)   *Cruising speed:* 190 mph (306 km/h)

The oldest Grumman amphibian. *Fully rounded tail planes and fin* and *twin engines* that *angle out* slightly away from the centerline of the aircraft.

The Goose is such an old design (built from 1937 to 1946) that many owners have changed such details as cockpit and fuselage windows. Many fly today with turboprops replacing the old radials and with retractable floats that fold up and become part of the wing surface in flight. But the angled-out engine position remains despite all other modifications. Crew of two and four to six passengers. Identifying the Goose is really dependent on recognizing its Grumman origins and its old-fashioned boatlike lines. The somewhat similar Grumman Widgeon is noticeably smaller, and the very rare Grumman Mallard has a distinctly upswept look to the rear fuselage. See those entries before deciding you've seen the Goose.

Republic
RC3 Seabee

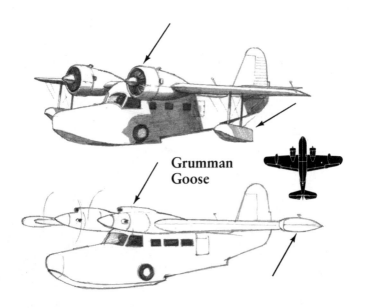

Grumman
Goose

Grumman G44 Widgeon

Length: 31'1" (9.47 m)   *Wingspan:* 40' (12.19 m)   *Cruising speed:* 130 mph (209 km/h) Mach 0.196

A small airplane with *in-line twin engines* mounted *parallel to aircraft midline;* sculpted Grumman-style fuselage.

Smallest of the twin-engine flying boats, the Widgeon saw extensive service as a patrol and antisubmarine craft in World War II. Although many have been converted to turboprops, the original Widgeon was sold with in-line engines, giving it a profile much different from the radial-engine Goose or Mallard. It is, in most respects, simply a scaled-down Goose, including the double-strut float mount; note, however, the less rounded tail fin and tail plane. Most of the 100 or so Widgeons still flying in North America have been converted by the McKinnon Company to turboprops and retractable wing-tip floats.

Grumman G73 Mallard

Length: 48'4" (14.73 m)   *Wingspan:* 66'8" (20.32 m)   *Cruising speed:* 180 mph (290 km/h)

Rare. *Large,* with noticeable *upswept rear fuselage* and very *high tail fin;* large *radial engines* and *solid float pylons.*

Only 59 ten-passenger Mallards were built between 1946 and 1951. Look for one of the few remaining Mallards in Louisiana's bayou country and in the Bahamas. Most of these will have conversions to turboprop engines: some have retractable floats. The only possible confusion is with the much larger (100-foot wingspan) Grumman Albatross (next entry). The Albatross fuselage is massive, compared to the Mallard, and all Albatross noses show a distinct, protruding radar dome. As a luxury flying yacht, the Mallard flew for persons as diverse as Henry Ford and King Farouk of Egypt.

Grumman G64 Albatross

Length: 61'3" (18.67 m)   *Wingspan:* 96'8" (29.46 m)   *Cruising speed:* 225 mph (362 km/h)

Scarce. *Very large,* with *twin radial engines;* sculpted, curving fuselage; *cantilever wing* (no struts).

Another "Grumman looking" aircraft, with solid pylons for the wing-tip floats and huge radial engines. The Albatross was built for air-sea rescue, patrol, and antisubmarine warfare. Note the nose radar dome, which is not seen on the smaller Grummans. The Canadair CL-215 (next entry) is almost as large as the Albatross, but, compared to a Grumman design, is all straight lines, whereas the Grummans have curves and shiplike moldings. Military versions were HU-16 in the U.S. Coast Guard, CSR-110 in the Canadian armed forces. Last military service was with U.S. Coast Guard; decommissioned in 1983.

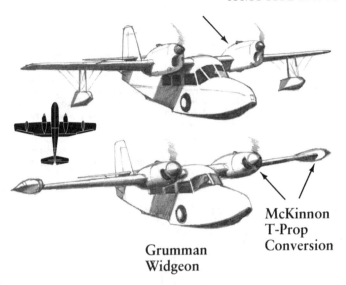

McKinnon
T-Prop
Conversion

Grumman
Widgeon

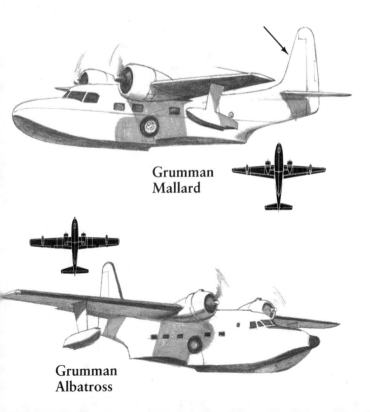

Grumman
Mallard

Grumman
Albatross

Canadair CL215 and refitted models

Specifications for factory model: *Length:* 65' (19.81 m)   *Wingspan:* 93'10" (28.6 m)   *Cruising speed:* 181 mph (291 km/h)

Rare but noticeable. A *huge, twin-engined* aircraft, with very *straight lines to the rear fuselage, wing and tail assembly;* compare the curved and angled silhouettes of the other twin amphibians.

The last amphibian to be produced, the CL215 was designed as a self-filling forest-fire water bomber and is seen most frequently in Canada. There are a few passenger and cargo versions flying, but no matter what configuration of windows and doors, the shape is unmistakable. Recent conversions (bottom sketch) have turboprops instead of radials and add end-plates to the wings. The fire-fighting version, now also used for oil field fires, is designed to make touch-and-go landings inland or at sea, scoop up 1500 gallons (5677 liters) of water while under way, and take off running for the fire. That's a payload of 6.25 tons (5.67 metric tons)!

Convair PBY-5 and PBY-6 Catalina

Length: 63'10" (19.50 m)   *Wingspan:* 104' (31.69 m)   *Cruising speed:* 130 mph (209 km/h)

Extremely rare. Huge *parasol wing* braced with *wing struts; twin radial engines.* The fuselage appears to hang suspended from the wing.

Although designed in 1935, the Catalina came equipped with retractable wing floats — something available only as postproduction modifications to Grumman flying boats. Most of the original PBYs were pure flying boats; most of the survivors are amphibious. Military PBYs had blister gun ports aft of the wings and a Plexiglas gun turret in the nose (or "bow"). The few civilian modifications still around have removed the forward gun turret, though a few kept the side blisters for sightseeing flights. The PBY-6, last of the series built, is identical to the PBY-5, except for a taller, thinner tail fin. A four-engine version, the Coronado, is no longer flying.

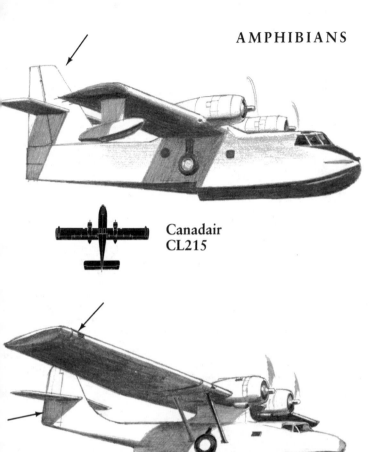

Canadair
CL215

Convair
Catalina, PBY-5

Wing D1 Derringer

Length: 23' (7.01 m)   *Wingspan:* 29'2" (8.89 m)   *Cruising speed:*
210 mph (338 km/h)

Very rare. A *very small twin: constant-chord* (equal depth) *wing; strongly swept tail fin; molded, one-piece side and windshield; rear window in cockpit roof.*

Exhibited at the Paris Air Show in 1971, a few produced from 1980 to 1985. It is of stretched metal construction, very sleek and rivetless. There was a prototype military version, intended as an inexpensive counterinsurgency plane for export to small countries. The only two-seat twin-propeller aircraft you will see.

Beech Duchess 76

Length: 29'1" (8.86 m)   *Wingspan:* 38' (11.58 m)   *Cruising speed:*
175 mph (282 km/h)

Quite common. Small twin; *three side windows; one-piece curved windshield; Hershey-bar T-tail plane and wing;* more *pointy-nosed* than the comparable Piper Seminole; *distinct bullet on tail plane; engine nacelles stop at wing's trailing edge.*

Beech's entrant in the small four-seater twin market, used for multi-engine training. First flown in 1974; first deliveries in 1977. The T-tail was extremely popular in the 1970s. Note the Piper Seminole and Cheyenne and the Beech Super King Air. The interest in T-tails was *perhaps* an affectation triggered by their wide use on jet airliners. Piper even added T-tails to existing single-engine models, the Lance and the Arrow. The Lance, however, reverted to a conventional tail, whereas the Arrow retained the T.

Piper PA44 Seminole

Length: 27'6" (8.39 m)   *Wingspan:* 38'7" (11.76 m)   *Cruising speed:* 192 mph (309 km/h)

A small, common twin. *T-tail; flattened engine nacelles extend slightly behind wing; two-piece windshield; three side windows of irregular geometry* (compare the small T-tail Beech Duchess 76 before deciding). The other two T-tail twins are much larger (see the Piper Cheyenne III and Beech Super King Air).

The Seminole (no relation to the U.S. Army "Seminole," their nickname for the military version of the Beech Queen Air) is a four-seat light transport and is popular as an inexpensive multi-engine trainer. Came in a turbocharged version that is identical on the exterior, but has an altitude ceiling of 20,000 feet and a pressurized cabin.

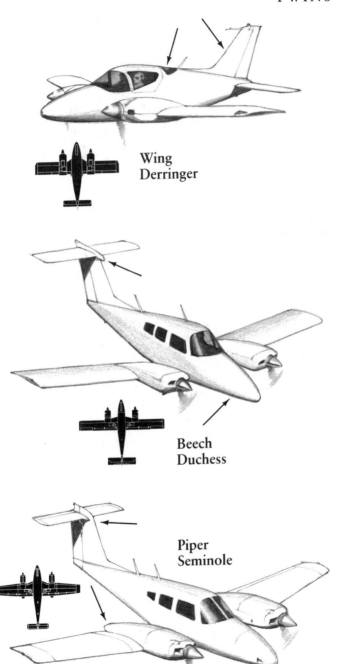

Wing
Derringer

Beech
Duchess

Piper
Seminole

Piper PA23 Apache

Length: 27'3" (8.30 m) *Wingspan:* 37' (11.28 m) *Cruising speed:* 150 mph (241 km/h)

Increasingly uncommon. *An old-fashioned small twin, rounded tail fin, tail planes and wing tips; two (rarely three) side windows; small engines set close to fuselage;* retracted wheels stay slightly exposed and are visible.

Built from 1954 to 1960, the first really light twin with economical engines; seats four. The wheels that do not quite retract are so built deliberately (as on many WWII bombers) — you can still land the plane if the system fails to extend the wheels; what's more, you can land, even if you forget to drop the wheels, without automatically demolishing the aircraft. Most restored models have higher horsepower engines and slightly higher cruising speeds. A few models were built with three side windows.

Piper PA23 Aztec, PA23-235 Apache

Length: 31'3" (9.52 m) *Wingspan:* 37'3" (11.35 m) *Cruising speed:* 204 mph (328 km/h)

A family of similar aircraft. *Conventional tail, low-wing twin; swept angular tail fin; three side windows;* noses vary in length from short (PA23-235 Apache) to medium (Aztec B, C) (top drawing) to long (Aztec D and later models). Seen overhead, the wing has complicated geometry: basically a Hershey-bar shape, but with added rounded wing tips and fairings from the fuselage to the leading edge of the wing at the engine nacelle, and from the outboard side of the engine nacelle into the wing's leading edge. The last model, the Aztec F (bottom drawing) has an angular outline to the wing tips, as though one had simply taken the old rounded shape and snipped it two or three times with a pair of shears.

Successor to the Apache (the first Aztec in 1960 was basically an Apache with a widened cabin to seat five and a new, angular, swept tail fin), the Aztec was a six-passenger twin available with turbocharged engines. An odd characteristic, occasionally useful as a field mark when the plane is overhead and going away, is that the tail fin and tail planes trail well behind the fuselage proper.

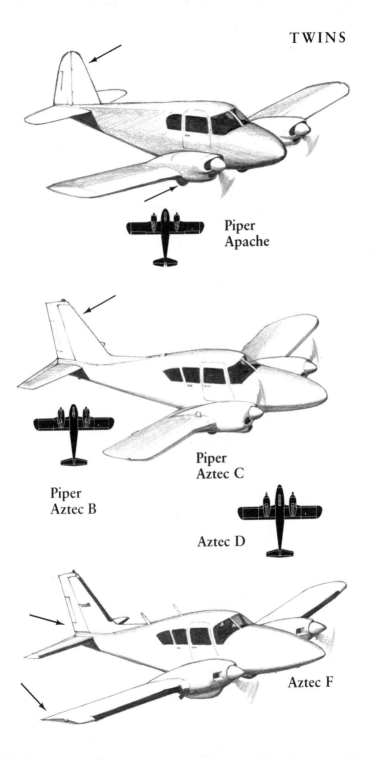

TWINS

Piper
Apache

Piper
Aztec C

Piper
Aztec B

Aztec D

Aztec F

Grumman American/Gulfstream American GA7, Cougar

Length: 29'10" (9.09 m)   *Wingspan:* 36'10" (11.23 m)   *Cruising speed:* 190 mph (306 km/h)

Not common; look for it at airports offering multiengine flight school. *Dihedral in wing and tail,* combined with *constant-chord* (equal width) *wing; three side windows; swept tail fin.*

First delivered in 1978, intended as an economical dual-control twin-engine trainer. Delivered as the Cougar with fancier interior. Seats four, including pilot and copilot or student. Production was sporadic, following the acquisition of Grumman American by American Jet Industries.

Piper PA34 Seneca

Length: 28'6" (8.69 m)   *Wingspan:* 38'11" (11.85 m)   *Cruising speed:* 187 mph (301 km/h)

A common sight. *Small low-wing twin; equal-chord* (width) *Hershey-bar wing and tail plane; swept tail fin.* Seneca III (illustrated) has wraparound windshield; Seneca II has a center windshield post; both have four side windows, each a different shape, diminishing to the rear. Seneca I had three larger side windows, each different in shape, and less streamlined engine nacelles. *The tail assembly seems stuck on as an afterthought:* The fin and tail planes stick out well aft of the end of the fuselage proper.

A popular five- or six-seat (including pilot) business and private aircraft. It essentially takes the single-engine Piper Cherokee SIX and substitutes two turbocharged engines. The test prototype was a Cherokee that retained the nose engine. It was flown, in fact, as a tri-motor, one of the last, and the briefest, pulling tri-motor flights in the history of aviation. Seneca III engines counter-rotate.

Piper PA60 Aerostar, Ted Smith Aerostar

Length: 34'10" (10.62 m)   *Wingspan:* 36'8" (11.18 m)   *Cruising speed:* 231 mph (372 km/h)

Not common, unique design. *A midwing twin; slight dihedral in wing, none in tail; leading edge of wing at right angle to fuselage, trailing edge tapers sharply to tip; tail plane strongly swept; bulbous-nosed; wraparound windshield, with two small windows above cockpit; fairing to tail fin is cut off abruptly.*

Ted Smith, a California designer, tried to build Aerostars from 1967 to 1978 in competition with the big three American builders. Although it's an attractive design and simple to construct, after several reorganizations, his company ended up as the Santa Maria Division of Piper. Typical of the Ted Smith touch, the three swept tail surfaces (fin and planes) and the three tail control surfaces are interchangeable.

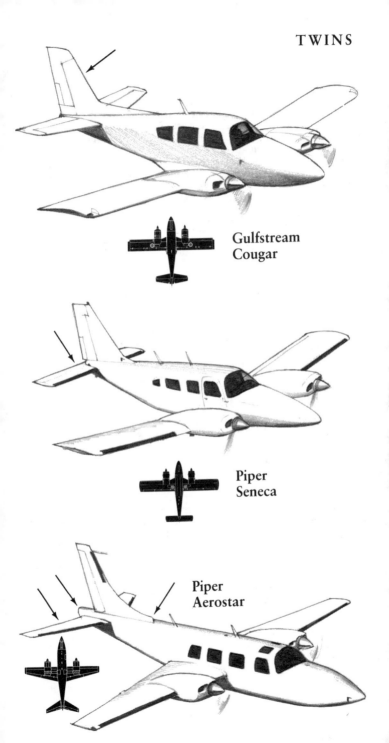

Gulfstream
Cougar

Piper
Seneca

Piper
Aerostar

Beech 50 Twin Bonanza, L-23 Seminole

Length: 31'6" (9.60 m)   *Wingspan:* 45'3" (13.80 m)   *Cruising speed:* 203 mph (327 km/h)

A series of *small, low-wing twins. Old-fashioned-looking vertical tail fin; dihedral in wing and tail; bulky engine nacelles house landing gear that does not retract fully.* As few as two side windows, as many as four, including the pilot's. But close at hand, note the unique *three-piece windshield,* with double divider strip in center.

Almost 1000 of these stubby little aircraft were produced from 1952 to 1961. It was the first civilian twin-engine plane available after WWII and opened up the corporate airplane market. Engine horsepower varied from 260 to 340. Could hold six passengers in seats three abreast in its chubby cockpit.

Beech 95 Travel Air

Length: 25'11" (7.90 m)   *Wingspan:* 37'10" (11.53 m)   *Cruising speed:* 195 mph (314 km/h)

Fairly common. *Very small low-wing twin; vertical tail fin; bulky nacelles; dihedral in wing, none in tail.* Landing gear retracts completely; compare Beech Twin Bonanza (previous entry). *One-piece windshield.* Close at hand, the triangular rear passenger window is unique, quite different from any Twin Bonanza.

Nearly 1000 of these little twins, the lowest priced on the market, were built from 1958 to 1968. The plane had a single-engine service ceiling of 4400 feet above sea level, which effectively eliminated it from the substantial airplane market of the Rocky Mountain and intermountain West, where airports are typically above 5000 feet.

Beech Baron D55, 58

Length: model 55, 28' (8.53 m); model 58, 29'10" (9.09 m)
Wingspan: both, 37'10" (11.53 m)   *Cruising speed:* both, 216 mph (348 km/h)

Common. A complex series of small *low-wing piston twins.* The consistent identification marks are the typical Beech wings, with a fairing from the wing root to the engine nacelle and *dihedral in wing, none in tail.* The 55 series had three side windows, the 58, four. The *windshield is set forward of the wing's leading edge on the model 58,* sometimes a useful field mark when the wing obscures the windows. A model 58 with turboprop engines, a swept tail plane and a taller tail fin is the rare, French-built Beech Marquis, a migrant from Europe.

A small four-place (three passengers, plus pilot) aircraft of considerable popularity. More than 6000 delivered since 1960, including a few hundred of the stretched model 58 since 1970. Regular improvements were in engines, air-conditioning, and avionics rather than in airframes.

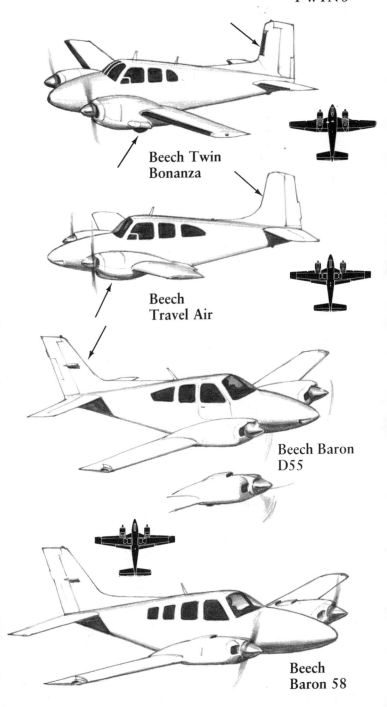

Beech Twin
Bonanza

Beech
Travel Air

Beech Baron
D55

Beech
Baron 58

Cessna T303 Crusader

Length: 30'5" (9.27 m)   *Wingspan:* 39' (11.90 m)   *Cruising speed:* 207 mph (333 km/h)

A *low-wing twin,* with the *tail plane mounted well up the fin; long engine nacelles trail behind wing; three rectangular passenger windows each side;* dihedral in wing, none in tail. Overhead, the wings and tail plane show symmetrical taper, with just a hint of the standard Cessna treatment: fairing from fuselage to wing's leading edge and from outboard side of engine nacelle to wing, but much less visible than on older Cessna twins.

Cessna's 1982 entry into the fuel-economic, easy-to-maintain, piston-engine business twin market. Long nose and trailing engine nacelles designed for baggage carrying. If you see it on the flight line, note that it's one of the few small twins with a stair built into the opening passenger door.

Beech B60 Duke

Length: 33'10" (10.31 m)   *Wingspan:* 39'3" (11.96 m)   *Cruising speed:* 250 mph (402 km/h)

A *low-wing twin piston* that shows *strong dihedral in wing and tail; long pointy nose; very strongly swept tail fin and tail plane; three rectangular windows each side.* Does not have the trailing oval passenger window typical of so many Beech aircraft; compare the Queen Air, King Air (page 110).

A four- or six-passenger plane with a crew of two, but was frequently sold as a top-of-the-line personal aircraft and seldom used in the passenger business. Delivered, since 1968, as a personal and corporate aircraft. It is easily recognized at a distance by its unique lines — the illusion of speed and a certain rakishness.

Rockwell (Fuji) Commander 700

Length: 39'5" (12 m)   *Wingspan:* 42'5" (12.93 m)   *Cruising speed:* 252 mph (405 km/h)

A *low-winged twin; unswept and level tail plane mounted partway up fin; slim wings with dihedral;* opposed-cylinder engines carried in *flattened nacelles well forward of the wing; air scoops under nacelles for turbochargers. Trapezoidal passenger windows* (three port, four starboard) *are absolutely unique.*

A joint design of Fuji in Japan and Rockwell International in the U.S., it was first flown in 1975. Seats four to six in pressurized cabin and has a crew of two. Its practical range is more than 800 miles (1300 km). One of the few light twins built that used NACA (National Advisory Committee on Aeronautics) wing designs, though the slim and symmetrically tapering wings were constructed entirely in Japan.

Cessna
Crusader

Beech
Duke

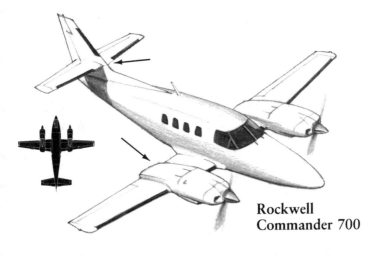

Rockwell
Commander 700

Piper PA31P-350 Mojave

Length: 34'6" (10.35 m)   *Wingspan:* 44'6" (13.35 m)   *Cruising speed:* 270 mph (434 km/h)

A 1983 introduction. A *low-wing twin,* with turbocharged engines in *very flattened nacelles that extend well behind the wing; dihedral in wing, none in tail; symmetrical taper both edges of wing and tail plane; three windows starboard, two port.*

A five-passenger luxury business plane with piston engines seems an odd introduction in the turboprop era, but the intent was fuel economy and a power plant that could be worked on without a doctorate in engineering. The cabin is unusually deep for a small twin and is reflected in the bulky fuselage carried well aft. The long nose is for baggage, as are the trailing engine nacelles.

Piper PA31 Navajo, Chieftain

A family of *low-wing twins,* with *flattened engine nacelles housing opposed six-cylinder engines; no tip-tanks;* all have characteristic Piper wing: *distinct leading edge fairing from fuselage to engine nacelle, both edges taper from nacelle to wing tip; dihedral in wing, none in tail plane. Note* that the newest Chieftain commuter (PA31-350 T1040) has turboprops in round nacelles that do not extend behind the wing—essentially like Cheyenne engines. Engine nacelles on the PA31-325 Navajo and PA31-350 Chieftain extend beyond trailing edge of wing. Nacelles on PA31 Navajo and the pressurized PA31P stop well short of the trailing edge. Navajos carry six passengers; Chieftains can accommodate up to ten.

Piper PA31-325 Navajo CR (main drawing)

Length: 32'7" (9.93 m)   *Wingspan:* 40'8" (12.40 m)   *Cruising speed:* 244 mph (393 km/h)

Three large and one small side window, not counting pilot's side window; counterrotating propellers; *nacelles extend beyond trailing edge.*

Piper PA31 and PA31P (center detail sketch)

PA31 is identical to PA31-325, except *engine nacelles do not extend past trailing edge.* PA31P (pressurized) has *three windows starboard, two port* (door on port side has no window).

Piper PA31-350 Chieftain

Length: 34'7" (10.55 m)   *Wingspan:* 40'8" (12.40 m)   *Cruising speed:* 251 mph (404 km/h)

The stretched Navajo is common in feeder airline and air-taxi service. *Shows five windows on each side, not counting pilot's window; nacelles on most models extend beyond trailing edge,* but the less common PA31-350-T1040 has turboprops in round nacelles that do not extend past trailing edge.

Piper
Mojave

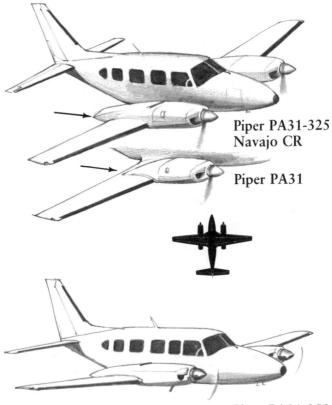

Piper PA31-325
Navajo CR

Piper PA31

Piper PA31-350
Chieftain

Piper PA31T Cheyenne

Length: Cheyenne IIXL, 36'8" (11.18 m)   *Wingspan:* all models,
42'8" (13.01 m)   *Cruising speed:* 244 mph (393 km/h)

Fairly common. *Low-wing turboprop twin; engine nacelles blend
into wing's trailing edge; swept tail fin; barely visible dihedral in
wing, none in tail; tip-tanks.* The XL model illustrated has four passenger windows starboard, three port. Earlier models Cheyenne I and
II are 2 feet shorter and show three- and two-passenger windows,
starboard and port. A few Cheyenne I's do not have tip-tanks.

Built after 1969, the high-powered Cheyenne II was actually the
typical and original Cheyenne. The Cheyenne I was a version with
less powerful engines and less standard equipment that was not introduced until 1978.

Piper PA30, PA39, Twin Comanche

Length: 25'2" (7.67 m)   *Wingspan:* 36'9" (11.22 m)   *Cruising
speed:* 186 mph (299 km/h)

A small *low-wing twin.* Manufactured *with and without tip-tanks;
engine nacelles stop well short of trailing edge.* Though it has the
characteristic Piper fairing from fuselage to engine nacelles, the leading edge is straight and the trailing edge tapered, which gives the
wing the illusion of *leaning forward. Dihedral in wing, none in tail
plane.* Comes with *two or* (more commonly) *three side windows, including the pilot's side window.*

A successful and popular series that first flew in 1962. All seat four
persons, including the pilot. Various models with turbo-charged engines, counter-rotating propellers, and internal layouts. Models with
tip-tanks somewhat resemble the Cessna 310, but 310 nacelles extend beyond trailing edge, 310 wing has no fairing between fuselage
and nacelles, and 310 shows two windows on each side, including
the pilot's.

Cessna 310, 320 Skyknight, U-3, L-27

Length: 29'7" (9.02 m)   *Wingspan:* 37'6" (11.43 m)   *Cruising
speed:* variable, about 177 mph (285 km/h)

A variety of popular aircraft sharing the minimum characteristics
of *twin engines on dihedral wing combined with level tail planes;
very flat engine nacelles; tip-tanks; distinct point at the bottom of the
tail fin.* Since 1969, there has also been a *noticeable ventral fin* (tail
skid). Rare Skyknight has four small side windows. Close at hand,
Cessna 310 and 320 tip-tanks are distinctly canted up and out from
the wing.

Cessna's entry into the business twin market quickly became a
military utility and liaison aircraft (U-3, L-27) and was produced
continuously from 1954 to 1982. Model changes tended to empha-
size minor changes in windows, streamlining, and engines. The 310s
with ventral fin and without rear windows date from 1969 to 1973.
The major change came in 1975, when the nose was lengthened and
a turbocharged engine became available. The turbo versions cruise at
more than 200 mph (322 km/h), and can be distinguished from the
conventional engines by the absence of a cowl flap on the bottom of
the nacelles.

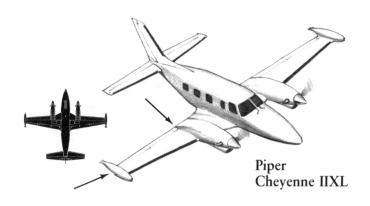

Piper
Cheyenne IIXL

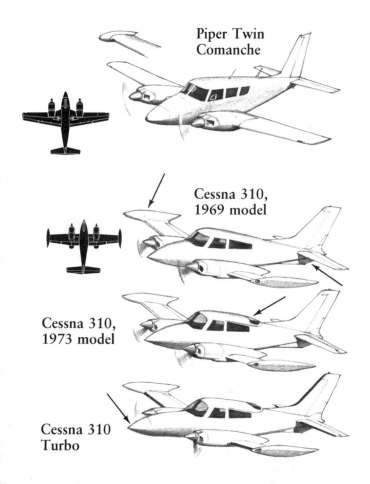

Piper Twin
Comanche

Cessna 310,
1969 model

Cessna 310,
1973 model

Cessna 310
Turbo

Cessna 340, 335

Length: 43'4" (10.46 m)   *Wingspan:* 38'1" (11.62 m)   *Cruising speed:* 212 mph (341 km/h)

A *low-wing twin. Four small oval windows each side; noticeable ventral fin: long-fuselaged and short-nosed* in its general aspect; *engine nacelles extend past trailing edge, tip-tanks are canted outward at a 30-degree angle; dihedral in wing, none in tail plane.* Overhead, it could be confused with the smaller Cessna 310. These two Cessnas have straight leading edges on wings that arise directly from the fuselage without any fairing there, or at the engine nacelles, and have tip-tanks.

This four-passenger, two-crew, pressurized aircraft has flown since 1971. The model 335 is not pressurized, but has exactly the same window layout, giving no external evidence of its not being able to operate at 30,000 feet, as the 340 can.

Cessna 411, 414 and 421A, 421B Golden Eagle

421A specifications: *Length:* 33'9" (10.29 m)   *Wingspan:* 39'11" (12.17 m)   *Cruising speed:* 226 mph (364 km/h)

A series of similar twins. Four or five passenger windows; *tip-tanks; long noses, no ventral fin; strong dorsal fin fairing to highly swept tail fin.* All have the typical Cessna wing, straight leading edge, slight taper of trailing edge beginning at engine nacelles. *Dihedral in wing, none in tail plane.* Detail below main drawing shows the unpressurized model, the 411; note the single side window for the pilot (pressurized models have a two-part side window).

Beginning in 1965, with the unpressurized Cessna 411, then in 1967, with pressurized versions, a series of six- to eight-passenger twins were built until 1985. The 414 is a less expensive, lower-powered version of the 421. Models built from 1965 to 1972 show four round windows. From 1973 to 1985, the 421 had five oval passenger windows; the 414 added the fifth window in 1974.

Cessna 414A Chancellor and 421C Golden Eagle

Chancellor specifications: *Length:* 36'4" (11.04 m)   *Wingspan:* 44'1" (13.44 m); Golden Eagle, 41' (12.5 m)   *Cruising speed:* 211 mph (339 km/h)

A pair of similar turbocharged twin piston planes. *Five oval windows; dihedral in wing, none in tail plane; without tip-tanks.* Very similar 414 Chancellor and 421A, 421B Golden Eagle are identical, except *with* tip-tanks. Compare the almost identical Cessna Corsair, Conquest I, which has everything as in 414A and 421C, except for a very sharp dihedral in tail, and turboprop engines. That one company should make so many very similar models is curious, and an annoyance to the viewer.

Cessna created two new models by dropping the characteristic tip-tanks from its Golden Eagle and Chancellor series in 1976 (while continuing to manufacture planes with tip-tanks). The new models, designated 414A Chancellor and 421C Golden Eagle, offered slightly better performance and some greater ease in managing the fuel systems.

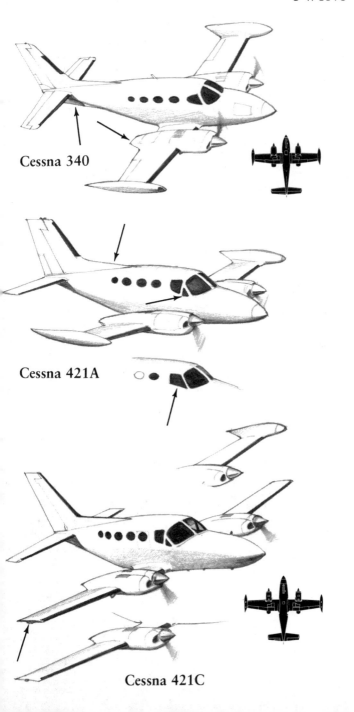

Cessna 340

Cessna 421A

Cessna 421C

Cessna 401, 402 Utiliner, Businessliner

Length: 36'1" (11 m) *Wingspan:* 39'10" (12.15 m) *Cruising speed:* 200 mph (322 km/h)

A *low-wing twin* with that Cessna look: *straight leading edge to wing; no fairing in wing at all; slight dihedral in wing, none in tail.* Models built from 1967 to 1971 (401, 402A, and early 402Bs) have four evenly spaced round windows that get smaller toward the tail. Models from 1971 to 1987 (later 402Bs and 402C) have five rectangular windows on each side, also tapering in size front to rear. All 402Bs have *tip-tanks* (see sketch).

Carrying a crew of one or two and six to nine passengers, Cessna Utiliners and Businessliners serve feeder lines and corporations. They aren't pressurized or particularly fast, but they were intended to be economical rather than exotic, as their sobriquets indicate.

Cessna 404 Titan, 406 Caravan II

Titan specifications: *Length:* 39'6" (12.04 m) *Wingspan:* 46'8" (14.23 m) *Cruising speed:* 230 mph (370 km/h)

The original Titan shows a *very strong 12-degree dihedral in tail* that separates it from the Cessna 401/402 (above), as does the number of passenger windows. Somewhat resembles the Conquests (next aircraft), but they have TV-screen (Conquest II) or oval porthole (Conquest I) windows, and they are both turboprops.

The last version of the Titan is the Cessna 406 Caravan II, which has an entirely different tail (see sketch), a low cross with no dihedral. Seen from the side, the Caravan II also has a distinct belly strake. In performance and efficiency, the Titan falls between the Businessliners and the Conquests, and is scarcer than either of them.

Cessna 441 Conquest (now Conquest II) and Cessna 425 Corsair (now Conquest I)

441 Conquest specifications: *Length:* 39' (11.89 m) *Wingspan:* 49' (14.94 m) *Cruising speed:* 290 mph (467 km/h)

Both aircraft are *low-wing twin turboprops. Very strong (12-degree) dihedral in tail plane.* Except for the engine and the dihedral in the tail, the 425 Corsair (Conquest I) is identical to the Cessna 421C Golden Eagle. Corsairs are scarcer than DC3s. Overhead, a typical Cessna wing, unfaired at wing root or nacelles. Turboprop engines on the much more common 441 Conquest (Conquest II) extend far forward of the straight leading edge, and do not show past trailing edge. Corsair (Conquest I) is similar, but it shows nacelle behind. Except when directly overhead, the dihedral will be very noticeable.

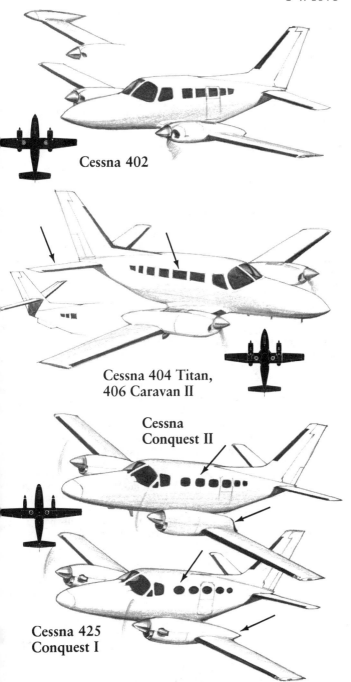

Cessna 402

Cessna 404 Titan,
406 Caravan II

Cessna
Conquest II

Cessna 425
Conquest I

Beech Queen Air, U-8, U-21 Seminole

Length: 35′6″ (10.82 m) *Wingspan:* 45′10″ (13.98 m) *Cruising speed:* 230 mph (370 km/h)

A series of midsized *low-wing twins. Matching 7-degree dihedrals in wing and tail; strongly swept tail fin; three and four rectangular windows, port and starboard, with trailing small oval window. Earliest models (B65) had vertical tail fin.*

Beginning with the Queen Air 65 in 1958, a long series of successful small twins with various engines. The matching dihedral is typical of both the Queen Air and the conventional-tail King Air and is an unusual combination.

Beech King Air A90-E90, A100, B100

Model E90 (includes U.S. Army U-21) specifications: *Length:* 35′6″ (10.32 m) *Wingspan:* 50′3″ (15.32 m) *Cruising speed:* 260 mph (418 km/h)

A series of *low-winged, twin turboprops with conventional tail. Slight dihedral in wings and tail plane.* Typical Beech window details: *no window in passenger door,* one smaller window bringing up the rear, *after a blank spot.* Stretched A100 is 4 feet longer than other models; has six large and one small window, starboard; and five large and one small, port side. Other models show four large windows, one small on starboard; three large, one small on port.

More than 1000 King Airs in service, the stretched A100 is a common feeder line 12-passenger plane. The other versions are six-passenger. Early King Airs were essentially pressurized Queen Airs with turboprop engines; easily distinguished overhead by the engine noise, on the ground by the round pressurized windows fitted in the same pattern as the Queen Air's square passenger windows.

Beech Super King Air B200, 350, 1300, T-44, U-12

B200 specifications: *Length:* 43′9″ (13.16 m) *Wingspan:* 54′6″ (16.6 m) *Cruising speed:* 320 mph (515 km/h)

A *low-winged twin turboprop with a T-tail.* Compare with Piper Cheyenne III (next page), and note that King Air has *round passenger windows, last one always smaller.* Don't rely on the standard Cheyenne tip-tanks; many Super King Airs have optional tip-tanks.

Developed in 1969, and gradually growing and improving since, although B200s are still produced. Earliest models showed four large windows each side, later models show five to seven, plus the trailing smaller window. The newer B350 has winglets, extra windows, and is 34 inches (0.85 m) longer. Rare B1300s have a cargo belly pod and ventral fins below the tail assembly. Common military VIP transport and twin-engine trainer.

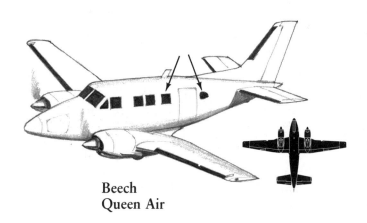

Beech
Queen Air

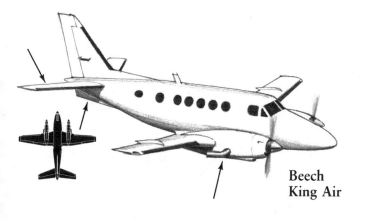

Beech
King Air

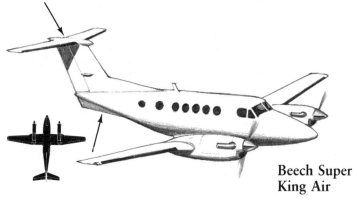

Beech Super
King Air

Piper PA42 Cheyenne III, IV

Length: 43'5" (12.24 m)   *Wingspan:* 47'8" (14.53 m)   *Cruising speed:* 318 mph (512 km/h)

A *business-size, low-wing twin turboprop with a T-tail, tip-tanks, and rectangular windows. Typical Piper wing, strong fairing wing root to nacelle.* (Compare the Beech Super King Air, which has optional tip-tanks and round windows.)

Cheyennes first flew in 1980, and are exceptionally fast turboprop business planes. One circled the world in 1982 in 88 hours of flying time, with 13 stops for fuel and rest. Executive seating for six, less comfortable arrangements for up to 11 passengers. The newer Cheyenne IV or 400 (see silhouette) has engine nacelles that *do not extend beyond the trailing edge of the wing.*

Cessna Skymaster 337, O-2

Length: 29'9" (9.07 m)   *Wingspan:* 38'2" (11.63 m)   *Cruising speed:* 173 mph (278 km/h)

Fairly common. One of two *smallish twin-boom planes you'll see;* compare with the military-only OV-1, page 170. The combination of *twin booms and in-line engines, one pushing, one pulling,* is unique.

More than 1200 337s fly in the United States and Canada. The original idea was to build a plane with twin-engine redundant safety that, in the case of the failure of one engine, would be simple to fly because the pilot would not have to compensate for the sudden and persistent torque of a wing-mounted, off-center engine. Cessna hoped that the U.S. government would permit single-engine-rated pilots to fly the 337. That was not allowed, and production stopped in 1980 except for a few, named the Reims Milirole, built in France. As the 0-2, more than 400 were in U.S. Army service.

Mitsubishi MU2 Marquise, Solitaire

Marquise specifications: *Length:* 39'5" (12.01 m)   *Wingspan:* 39'2" (11.94 m)   *Cruising speed:* Marquise, 340 mph (547 km/h); Solitaire, 370 mph (595 km/h)

A fairly common, *small, high-wing twin turboprop. Tip-tanks; tail plane set noticeably lower than wings.* Earlier Japanese-built *Marquise has bulging fuselage fairings to hold retractable wheels.* American-assembled *Solitaire has smooth fuselage into which gear retracts.* Early Japanese Marquise models are 33 feet long; all American Solitaires are also 33 feet.

A moderately popular corporate plane. The relatively high cruising speed, combined with fuel efficiency and room for four to nine passengers, made it the hot-rod of twin turbos. It even became a popular plane to steal and use in the Caribbean drug-smuggling underground. Several models (the plane comes with a variety of engines) have ranges up to 1680 miles (2700 km), which is long for the class.

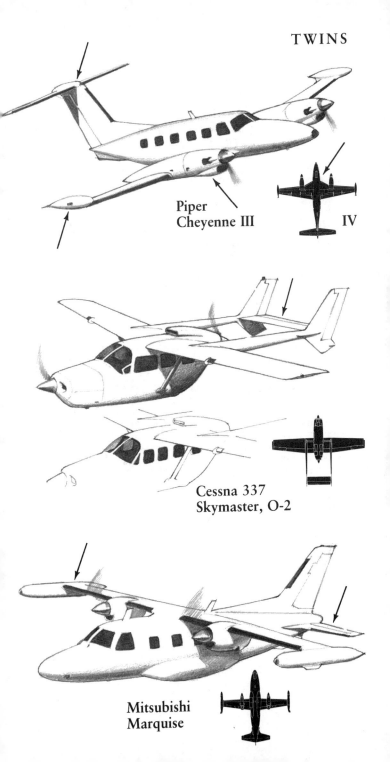

TWINS

Piper
Cheyenne III   IV

Cessna 337
Skymaster, O-2

Mitsubishi
Marquise

Partenavia P-68C

Length: 31'4" (9.55 m)   *Wingspan:* 39'5" (12 m)   *Cruising speed:*
185 mph (298 km/h)

Rare in North America. A very *sleek and long-nosed high-wing twin with fixed gear and wheel fairings.* Seen directly overhead, it could be confused with the much larger de Havilland Twin Otter, as both have *constant chord wings and tail planes.* But note the Partenavia's *unusual bracing fillet from fuselage to leading edge of tail plane/horizontal stabilizer.*

The remaining Partenavias (fewer than 50 at this writing) in North America are generally used by flight schools as dual-control twin-engine trainers. Many more in Italy, where a bubble-nosed version is a police and search-and-rescue vehicle.

Gulfstream and Rockwell Commander, Shrike Commander, Aero Commander, etc.

Aero Commander 520 specifications: *Length:* 34'6" (10.52 m)
Wingspan: 44'7" (13.60 m)   *Cruising speed:* 197 mph (317 km/h)
Turbo Commander 690 specifications: *Length:* 44'4" (13.51 m)
Wingspan: 46'8" (14.22 m)   *Cruising speed:* 288 mph (463 km/h)
Shrike Commander (Aero Commander 500U) specifications: *Length:*
35'1" (10.69 m)   *Wingspan:* 49'2" (15 m)   *Cruising speed:*
201 mph (323 km/h)

A complex family of airplanes. Began in 1948 with the four-passenger piston-engine Aero Commander and proceeded through the turboprop Rockwell 690 and Gulfstream 840, 900, 980 and 1000, 1200 series, carrying as many as ten passengers. All share certain characteristics: *high wing with slight dihedral, twin engines, strong dihedral in tail planes.* Models with turboprops from 690B on have small winglets. Very earliest four-passenger Aero Commanders and Shrike Commanders have a curved leading edge to the tail fin; all later models, a straight-edged, strongly swept tail fin. Another characteristic, from the Aero Commander on, is the *upswept fuselage,* which becomes increasingly distinct as the later models appear. Long-nosed and streamlined, compared to other high-wing twins. The streamlining effect is visually enhanced by the dihedrals in wing and tail plane. The authors accept the judgment of other airplane aficionados who lump the whole, varied, 25-year-old class of airplanes under the single category: Commanders.

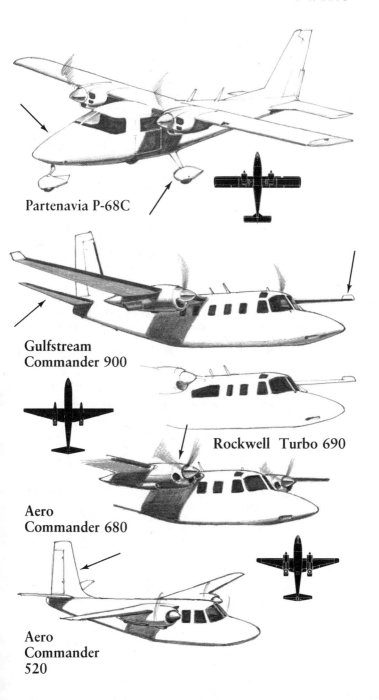

Partenavia P-68C

Gulfstream
Commander 900

Rockwell Turbo 690

Aero
Commander 680

Aero
Commander
520

de Havilland DHC6 Twin Otter

Length: 51'9" (15.77 m)   *Wingspan:* 65' (19.81 m)   *Cruising speed:* 200 mph (322 km/h)

Slim-bodied, with *long, thin high wings* and *twin turboprops; fixed gear; conventional tail; wing braced from fuselage at landing gear root.* Compare somewhat similar and much rarer GAF Nomad (below), whose wing brace rises from the landing gear itself.

Built from 1965 to 1988, it's one of the most popular small airline and air-taxi planes ever flown. More than 600 are in service. Carries 14 to 18 passengers in a fairly quiet, center-aisle cabin. Very short takeoff and landing qualities; can take off across the width of most airports. Seen as a float plane, though not as often as the de Havilland single-engine Otter.

Pilatus Britten-Norman Islander BN-2, Trislander MK III

Islander specifications: *Length:* 35'8" (10.87 m)   *Wingspan:* 49' (14.94 m)   *Cruising speed:* 150 mph (241 km/h)

A plane of odd geometry. *Fuselage rectangular in cross section; varied window shapes,* rectangular, trapezoidal, rhomboid; *Hershey-bar wing and tail; curved wing tips* are auxiliary fuel tanks; *double wheels* on *lumpy nonretractable landing gear.*

Designed for fuel-efficient, low-speed, low-density commuter routes. The earlier versions had a short nose; whereas the last version, the Trislander, has a longer fuselage, a T-tail, and a third engine mounted high on the tail fin. A low-technology airplane, it has been manufactured under license in Romania and assembled from supplied parts in the Philippines and the U.S. Seats up to 18 passengers and a single pilot; no aisle, entry through doors directly to seats.

GAF (Government Aircraft Factory, Australia) Nomad

Length: 41'2" (12.56 m); long-nosed model N24, 47'1" (14.36 m)   *Wingspan:* 54'2" (16.51 m)   *Cruising speed:* 193 mph (311 km/h)

Rare in North America. *High wing, twin turboprops; tail plane mounted partway up tail fin; wing struts rise out of the wheel pants of the fixed landing gear* (compare the de Havilland Twin Otter strut and tail).

Developed by the Australian factory as a military search and rescue and light transport in 1971. Two civil versions: the short-nosed N22 for 12 passengers, the long-nosed N24 for 15. Competitive in the same market as the DHC Twin Otter and, as such, may be seen fitted with floats. Several have been ordered by North American air taxis and commuter airlines.

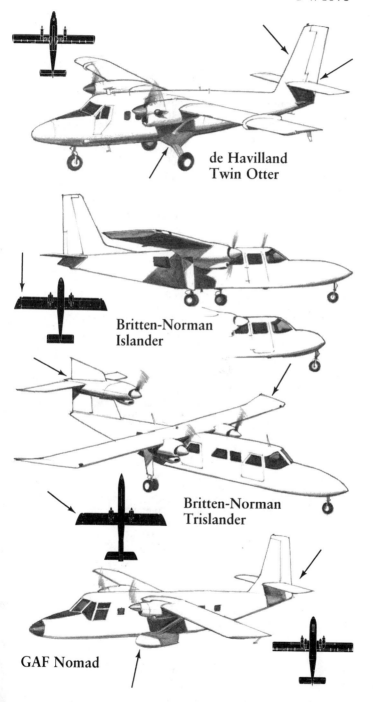

TWINS

de Havilland
Twin Otter

Britten-Norman
Islander

Britten-Norman
Trislander

GAF Nomad

CASA C212 Aviocar

Length: 49'10" (15.2 m) *Wingspan:* 62'4" (19 m) *Cruising speed:* 196 mph (315 km/h)

Still rare. *Stubby look, high wings, twin turboprops, upswept rear fuselage, conventional tail, nonretractable gear.* Compare equally stubby Shorts Skyvan (below), which has braced wing and unswept fuselage, or de Havilland Dash 8 (next page), which is upswept but has T-tail and retractable gear.

CASA is Spain's aircraft manufacturer, and the Aviocar is their design. Originally, a 16-man paratroop transport and utility freighter or air ambulance. The civil versions can carry 19 passengers and operate from the shortest and roughest of airstrips. A popular commuter aircraft in the Far East and African countries, where it replaces the aging WWII-surplus planes that have ended their careers in Third World airlines.

Shorts Skyliner, Skyvan

Length: 40'1" (12.22 m) *Wingspan:* 64'11" (19.79 m) *Cruising speed:* 173 mph (278 km/h)

Stubby, fixed landing gear with wheels tucked up under body; *twin tail fins; long, thin wings with braces.*

Resembling a flying bathtub with a thin wing glued on the top, the Short Brothers Skyvans serve small airlines in eastern North America and Alaska. The plane, built of a metal-resin composite with little or no insulation, seems remarkably noisy to passengers who took to flying after the DC3 era. More than 150 Skyvans (or more luxuriously appointed Skyliners) were built from 1964 to 1982.

Shorts 330, C-23 Sherpa, 360

Length: 58' (17.69 m) *Wingspan:* 74'8" (22.67 m) *Cruising speed:* 173 mph (278 km/h)

Bizarre configuration: *long, thin, untapered wing* with *large strut; semiretractable wheels* show even in flight. Most models have a *double tail fin,* like their brother, the Shorts Skyvan (above). One is not surprised that the builder, Short Brothers Company, was once a leading manufacturer of flying boats.

Introduced in 1976 as a fuel-efficient feeder airliner, the 30-seat Shorts 330 is of composite metal and resin construction; very light weight and low maintenance. A slightly larger version, the Shorts 360, carrying 36 passengers and bearing a conventional tail, has been purchased by several North American commuter airlines. A variant 330 is used by U.S. forces in Europe for shuttling between bases.

TWINS

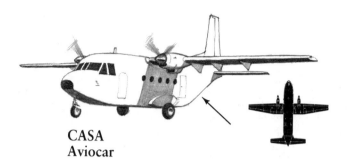

CASA
Aviocar

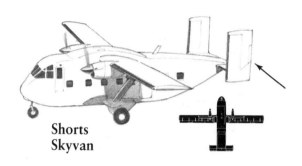

Shorts
Skyvan

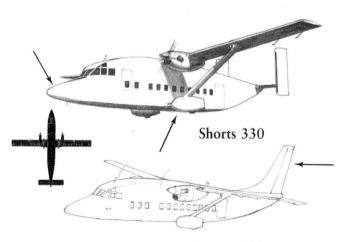

Shorts 330

Shorts 360

Dornier 228, Series 200

Length: 54'4" (16.56 m)   *Wingspan:* 55'8" (16.97 m)   *Cruising speed:* 266 mph (428 km/h)

Not common, but heavily used as a feeder airline, and so, commonly seen. *Long-nosed, the high-tech wing shape somewhat resembles the Islander/Trislander series but with very short engine nacelles; boxy, bumpy fuselage shape.*

If you set out to build a small, slow, durable, economical short-haul airliner and you didn't much care what it looked like, you'd get a Dornier. Travelers to Europe and Africa will see an occasional 228 in military camouflage, or dressed up with radar pods for marine surveillance.

Aerospatiale (Nord) 262, Mohawk 298

Length: 63'3" (19.28 m)   *Wingspan:* 71'10" (21.90 m)   *Cruising speed:* 233 mph (375 km/h)

Rare, local. *High, thin, tapering wings; bulging landing gear nacelles on fuselage; tires exposed even when retracted.*

This 26-passenger short-haul airliner went into service in 1963 and, with improved engines, has survived into the 1980s. It was one of the first of the high-efficiency, short-distance airliners, and was soon surpassed by later models (the Shorts 300, for example). Only 110 were built; perhaps a dozen still carry passengers.

de Havilland DHC8 Dash 8

Length: 75'6" (23.01 m)   *Wingspan:* 84' (25.6 m)   *Cruising speed:* 280 mph (451 km/h)

Rare. Twin turboprops that extend well before and behind a high wing; upswept rear fuselage combined with T-tail, retractable landing gear.

A little brother (32 passengers) of de Havilland's successful four-engined Dash 7. Slight dihedral in the wings, combined with the wide-span tail plane, gives the Dash 8 some of the elegance of the Dash 7. It is designed with slow-rotation, four-bladed propellers and new turbo engines to operate as quietly as possible from urban airports. A few in U.S. military. New Series 300 is an 11'3" (3.43 m) stretch.

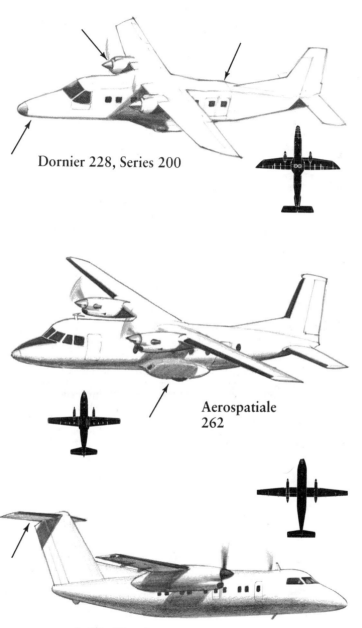

Dornier 228, Series 200

Aerospatiale
262

de Havilland
Dash 8

Aérospatiale/Aeritalia ATR 42, ATR 72

ATR 42 specifications: *Length:* 74'5" (22.67 m)   *Wingspan:* 80'8"
(24.57 m)   *Cruising speed:* 279 mph (450 km/h)

Few in number, but constantly in use as airline feeder, so, *visually
common. Huge sweeping tail fin to a high-cross, almost-T-tail;* fuselage tapers to a *tail cone* (a close-out fairing); *very large landing-gear
fairing under fuselage.*

Roughly the same size and configuration as a de Havilland Dash 8,
the ATR is heavier-looking, thanks to the landing gear fairings and
tail fin. A newer model, the ATR 72, is a *very large high-wing twin,*
a 15 foot (4.57 m) stretch of the ATR 42, but visual outlines and shapes
are identical.

Fokker F27, Fokker 50 Friendship

Fokker 50 specifications: *Length:* 82'10" (25.25 m)   *Wingspan:*
95'2" (29 m)   *Cruising speed:* ??

Not as long-nosed as the Dornier, and much larger. The Fokker
F27 (illustrated) is typical: *Long fairing to tail parallels the upsweep
of the rear fuselage; pointy-nosed, long engine nacelles extend symmetrically ahead and behind wing.*

The new Fokker 50 is a higher-performance, modern-materials version of the old F27 and stretch F227. If you catch a 50 sitting on the
runway, engines off, it will show a six-bladed propeller, and its windows are more TV-screen-shaped than the oval F27 and F227. A
fairly common feeder airliner.

Fairchild C-119 Flying Boxcar

Length: 89'5" (27.25 m)   *Wingspan:* 109'3" (33.30 m)   *Cruising
speed:* 200 mph (km/h)

Rare, and probably parked; a bathtub body with a twin-boom tail.
None in military service. If you're watching World War II news-
reels and you think you see a C-119, it is probably the predecessor
C-82 "Packet." C-119s were heavily used during the Korean War,
and some in Vietnam, mostly as gunships. Just to confuse things, a few
C-119s with jet-assisted takeoff were called C-119 Packets. Very few
hours flown today, but many are parked around the United States.

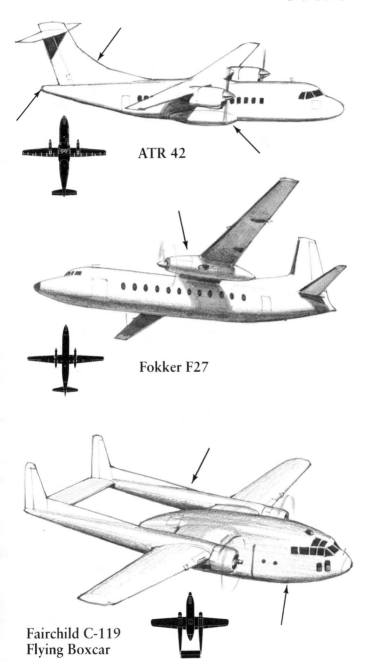

ATR 42

Fokker F27

Fairchild C-119
Flying Boxcar

Swearingen (Fairchild) Merlin II

Length: 40'1" (12.22 m)   *Wingspan:* 45'11" (14 m)   *Cruising speed:* 295 mph (475 km/h)

Small and fairly common. *Low wing, conventional tail, turboprops.* Resembles a smoother, bulkier, more streamlined Beech Queen Air. *Three rather large rectangular windows on each side.*

Swearingen, a company that specialized in putting turboprops, streamlined fairings and pressurization into other companies' production aircraft, took the Queen Air wing and built a streamlined, pressurized fuselage for it from scratch. The small number of fairly large windows is unusual in a pressurized aircraft. Compare the Beech King Air (five or six small windows) or the Cessna Conquest (six small windows) for conventional treatment of similarly sized aircraft.

Swearingen (Fairchild) Merlin III, Fairchild 300

Length: 42'2" (12.85 m)   *Wingspan:* 46'3" (14.10 m)   *Cruising speed:* 288 mph (463 km/h)

Common. Combines *low symmetrically tapering wing* with *strongly swept tail plane mounted midway up and well forward on the tail fairing.* Compare larger Merlin IV (next entry). Similarly configured Handley Page Jetstream 31 has unswept tail plane mounted farther back on the fin and shows seven small round windows. The midtailed Rockwell Commander 700 has trapezoidal windows, unswept tail plane and, unlike the Merlin or the Jetstream, has no ventral fin at all.

A popular series of executive turboprops. Some early Merlin IIIs have only three or four windows to a side, and a variety of turboprop engines have been mounted on the same basic airframe. The strong dorsal and ventral fins shown on the Merlin and the Handley Page Jetstream are intended to improve handling when the plane is forced to fly on one engine. The 1984 Fairchild 300 has winglets.

Fairchild Merlin IVA, Metro III, Fairchild 400

Length: 59'4" (18.08 m)   *Wingspan:* 46'3" (14.10 m)   *Cruising speed:* 279 mph (449 km/h)

Common. Combines *low, symmetrically tapered wings and strongly swept tail plane mounted well forward on the tail fin fairing.* Compare the much smaller Merlin IIIB (previous entry).

Carrying 12 passengers in the Merlin IV executive cabin or up to 20 passengers in the Metro airliner cabin, this Swearingen-designed airplane has seen some use in the U.S. Midwest as a commuter airliner. It is quite rare as an executive plane. Some 300 delivered worldwide since 1971. The 1983 models introduced winglets; the Merlin IV was renamed Fairchild 400 in 1984. New Merlin and Metro V have T-tail.

Swearingen
Merlin II

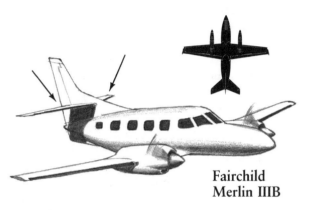

Fairchild
Merlin IIIB

Fairchild
Metro III

Beech 99 Airliner

Length: 44'7" (13.59 m)   *Wingspan:* 45'10" (13.97 m)   *Cruising speed:* 270 mph (434 km/h)

A common and variable aircraft. Combines *low wing with two turboprop engines, conventional tail, and distinct ventral fin.* Unfortunately, it has to be distinguished from similar planes, including its predecessor, the Beech Queen Air, by *noting the window patterns.* The 99s show, from the front, one small rectangular window; five or six larger rectangular windows; the typical Beech gap on or opposite the passenger door; and a small oval window at the rear.

There are a couple of hundred of the 15-passenger stretched and pressurized version of the Beech Queen Air in service with dozens of small airlines. Built since 1965, with a couple of engine variations. A rather ordinary-looking aircraft, with a moderately swept tail fin (compared to the Queen Air) and a long, pointy nose.

Embraer EMB110 Bandeirante

Length: 47'10" (14.58 m)   *Wingspan:* 50'3" (15.32 m)   *Cruising speed:* 203 mph (327 km/h)

An increasingly common commuter airliner. *Low-winged; twin turboprops; in the air, a strong impression of rectangularity: Note the sharp extension of the tail fin down through the tail plane to a ventral fin; overhead, slightly tapering wing and tail planes look quite rectangular; engines with deep nacelles* (to hold landing gear) *extend very far forward of the wing.* The wraparound *cockpit windows are composed of eight separate panes,* which is most unusual in recently built aircraft. The 1984 model has a dihedral in tailplane.

A 17- to 19-passenger unpressurized aircraft first delivered to the U.S. in 1976. The Bandeirante competes directly with such small commuter airliners as the Beech 99. The parent company, Empresa Brasilia de Aeronautica, builds single- and twin-engine Piper airplanes under license; it also manufactures components for Northrop's F-5 fighters.

Embraer EMB120 Brasilia

Length: 64'5" (19.64 m)   *Wingspan:* 74'10" (19.76 m)   *Cruising speed:* 288 mph (463 km/h)

A 1984 introduction. *Very large low-wing twin turboprop* with *T-tail* (of twin T-tails, compare the much smaller Piper Seminole, Duchess, Cheyenne III, and Beech Super King Air). The only other large twin T-tail is the *high-winged* de Havilland DHC8 Dash 8. High overhead, they might be confused if you do not pay attention to the wing placement.

Ordered by commuter airlines from coast to coast, this 30-passenger airliner includes state-of-the-art technology. The fuel-efficient Canadian-built turboprops have an unusual feature: fully disengageable propellers, so that the engines can be run at the loading gate. This feature allows passengers to load while keeping the air-conditioning and heating systems on, as it does getting back in the air without delays associated with engine starting.

Beech 99
Airliner

Embraer
Bandeirante

Embraer
Brasilia

Handley Page and British Aerospace Jetstream 31

Length: 47'1" (14.35 m)   *Wingspan:* 52' (15.85 m)   *Cruising speed:* 269 mph (433 km/h)

Not common. Combines *low wing, turboprops, unswept tail plane mounted well up on tail fin, modest fairing to tail fin, and seven small round windows on each side.* (Newest version, the BAe Jetstream 31, has a *distinct ventral fin.* Compare the Merlin IVA, with distinct dorsal fin/tail fairing, of which some early models had ten small round windows.

The venerable Handley Page Company went broke in 1970 after designing and building the prototype of the successful Jetstream. It is now built by the Scottish division of British Aerospace. Handley Page types (illustrated) show a much longer propeller spinner than the current production model 31, with Garrett turboprops. Each carries 18 passengers.

Beech 1900 Airliner, 1900D

Length: 57'9" (17.60 m)   *Wingspan:* 54'6" (16.61 m)   *Cruising speed:* 280 mph (451 km/h)

Combines *low wing with T-tail fuselage-mounted stabilons just forward of tail;* typical Beech wing begins with *rectangular section from fuselage to engine; trailing edge tapers to tip more sharply than leading edge.*

A 19-passenger aircraft intended for commuter routes requiring frequent stops. The sharp dihedral in the low wing, combined with the T-tail, gives the 1900 a unique appearance in the landing and takeoff pattern. Note also the very large double engine exhausts. The 1900D is a "tall body" with stand-up headroom.

Saab-Scania 340A Commuter

Length: 63'9" (19.43 m)   *Wingspan:* 70'4" (21.44 m)   *Cruising speed:* estimated, 300 mph (483 km/h)

A fairly conventional-looking airplane: *Tall, swept tail fin, strongly dihedral tail plane; deep fuselage is carried full depth well aft; unusual engine nacelles, which are narrow and deep, rise high above and show well below wing.*

A 34-passenger airliner with wings and tail by Fairchild, the rest by Saab; assembled in Sweden. The aspect of the plane is unique — strong dihedrals in tail planes tend to be unusually noticeable, as on the old Martin 404. The bulky body and slim wing will attract attention. Saab-Scania may build a stretch to 85' (25.91 m).

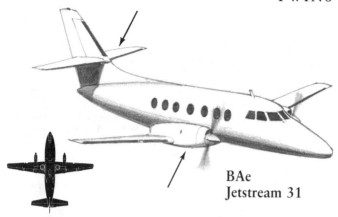

BAe
Jetstream 31

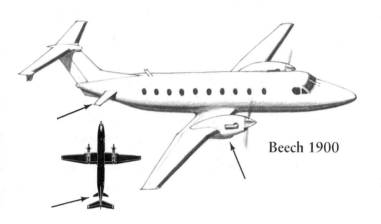

Beech 1900

Saab
340A

Grumman American G159 Gulfstream I

Length: 64'8" (19.72 m)   *Wingspan:* 78'4" (23.88 m)   *Cruising speed:* 288 mph (463 km/h)

Not common. *Slim-winged; short-nosed; distinct swelling under engine nacelles* houses landing gear. A stretched version, the G159 1C, is 10 feet longer and shows seven, rather than five, oval passenger windows.

Carrying 24 passengers in the short version, or 37 in the model 1C stretch, some 200 of these durable, but not particularly fuel-efficient, corporate planes operate in North America. Though built from 1960, with the stretching done in the early 1980s, they're not currently competitive with newer aircraft of the same capacity.

British Aerospace 748

Length: 67' (20.42 m)   *Wingspan:* 102'5" (31.22 m)   *Cruising speed:* 281 mph (452 km/h)

One of two modern *twin turboprops* that share the characteristic of *massive bulges on the bottom of the nacelles* (to house landing gear). Compare the Japanese NAMC YS11, next page. The BAe 748 has *strong wing dihedral, beginning at fuselage,* combined with *horizontal tail planes.* Convair 640 has similar wing and tail configuration but without the massive landing gear fairings. Passenger BAe 748s have ten large rounded windows. The NAMC has many small, square windows.

A stretched 748 ATP has much less bulbous engine/landing gear nacelles, and 26 windows on its much longer fuselage, 85'4" (26 m) overall.

Convair CV240, 340, 440, 540, 580, 600, 640

CV580 specifications: *Length:* 81'6" (24.84 m)   *Wingspan:* 105'4" (32.11 m)   *Cruising speed:* 300 mph (483 km/h)

A variety of highly similar *twin-engine, low-wing* airliners, with *slight dihedral in wing, and horizontal tail planes.* In the U.S. and Canada, most are *turboprop conversions,* series 540 to 640. (CV580 is the most common.) Except for the engine nacelles, very similar to the BAe HS748 and NAMC YS11. Whether old piston or new turboprop, *the nacelles are slim* compared to the bulging, landing-gear-holding nacelles on the HS748 and YS11.

The original 240, 340, 440 series, seating 40 to 50 passengers, with Pratt and Whitney radials, have been supplanted for the most part by turboprop conversions. A few made-from-scratch turboprops produced by Canadair — the Canadair CC-109 — are still in service as troop carriers in the Canadian armed forces. Model numbers reflect little except the time of manufacture or re-engining. However, the 340 and 440 were slightly stretched versions of the original 240.

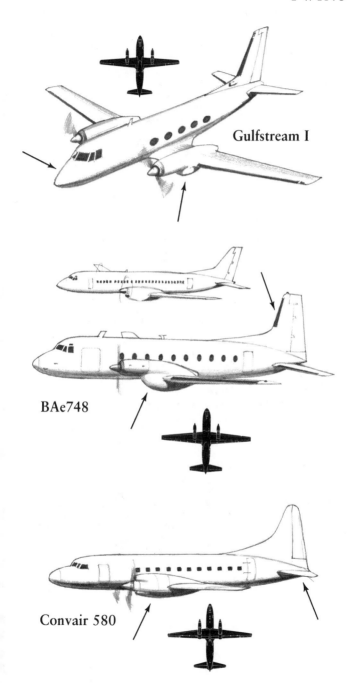

Gulfstream I

BAe748

Convair 580

NAMC YS11

Length: 86'3" (26.30 m)   *Wingspan:* 104'11" (32 m)   *Cruising speed:* 281 mph (452 km/h)

Not common, but seen especially in Alaska and in the southwestern U.S. *Massive landing gear fairings under nacelles* (compare the BAe 748), *slight dihedral wing; horizontal tail plane; dozens of tiny, rectangular windows.*

Either the limits of conventional airplane design were reached in the 1950s or this is a virtual copy of the British Aerospace 748. Its design was begun in 1960, a year after the 748 went to the drawing board. The YS11 does carry 60 passengers, not 44, but is otherwise highly similar to the BAe 748; the windows are the most obvious difference.

Curtiss C-46 Commando

Length: 76'4" (23.27 m)   *Wingspan:* 108' (32.92 m)   *Cruising speed:* 235 mph (378 km/h)

A rare survivor. (Make sure it's not a DC3 before deciding.) *The plane with no nose; greenhouse cockpit windows;* the wings are like the DC3's, strongly tapered on the leading edge, straight on the trailing edge. Unlike the DC3, has *fully retractable landing gear* and is larger, bulkier than DC3.

Developed as a 36-passenger airliner in 1940 to compete with the DC3, it was built as only a military transport. A few dozen still survive with small, poor regional airlines; likeliest to be seen in the Caribbean, southwestern Alaska, along the Mexican border. It's not nearly so common as the somewhat similar DC3.

Douglas DC3, C-47, Dakota

Length: 64'5" (19.65 m)   *Wingspan:* 95' (28.96 m)   *Cruising speed:* 194 mph (312 km/h)

Not common, but widely distributed. A *tail-dragger* that sits nose up on the flight line; in the air, *very short-nosed look,* as the wings are set well forward and the large radials flank the cockpit area; wing tapers on the leading edge only; *tires of forward landing gear do not retract out of sight; tail wheel is nonretractable.*

First built in 1935 and flown the world over, with several hundred surviving long after the assembly shut down in 1946. Seated 36 in unpressurized discomfort, as many as 50 in its troop-carrying configuration. Still flying passengers in all parts of North America, with hundreds parked on airfields and making occasional unscheduled freight trips. A few still in government service in Canada. As with many aircraft with partially retractable wheels, the purpose is to allow for a relatively safe landing in the event that the gear is not, or cannot be, lowered.

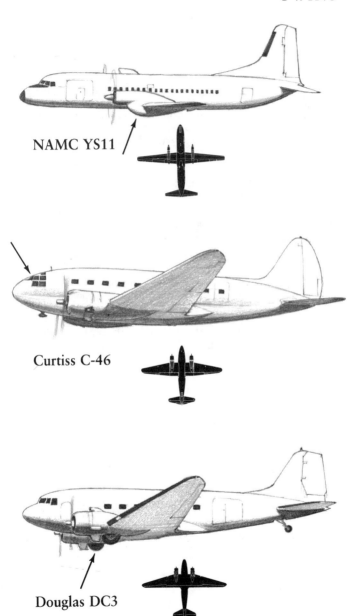

NAMC YS11

Curtiss C-46

Douglas DC3

de Havilland DH104 Dove, Riley Turbo-Exec Dove

Length: 39'4" (12 m)   *Wingspan:* 57' (17.37 m)   *Cruising speed:* 162 mph (261 km/h)

Extraordinarily rare. *Long, tapering wings; engines mounted well forward on the wing; distinctive bump over cockpit* gives crew stand-up headroom. Originals show a conventional curved tail, whereas Riley turbo-charged conversions have a swept, angular tail fin.

About 600 built by de Havilland between 1946 and 1968, many as military light transports. They became a popular executive aircraft after WWII, and the turbo conversions continue to fly in general aviation. A Dove with the old Gipsy Queen engines is a real rarity in North America. The first one you see is likely to be the last one.

Beech 18, C-45

Length: 35'2" (10.72 m)   *Wingspan:* 49'8" (15.14 m)   *Cruising speed:* 185 mph (298 km/h)

Still common, but highly variable. Twin-engine, low-wing, *distinctive Beech twin tail:* Note that *tail plane does not extend through fins.* Seen with rounded (early) and squared-off (late model) wing tips.

The durable Beech 18 was built from 1937 to 1972, with thousands in WWII as C-45s. It has been refitted in a bewildering variety of forms: with tricycle gear to replace the semiretractable tail-dragging gear; in stretched versions; in long-nosed models; with turboprop engines; with conventional rather than double-fin tails; and in one bizarre case, with a T-tail. *The odd window pattern — a long, rectangular passenger window surrounded by two smaller square windows — is always a good field mark.* The last production 18s were sold to Japan Airlines.

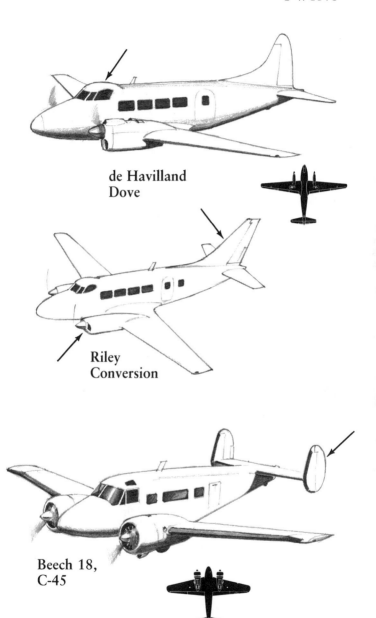

de Havilland
Dove

Riley
Conversion

Beech 18,
C-45

Lockheed 10, and 12 "Electra Jr."

Model 12 specifications: *Length:* 36'4" (11.07 m)   *Wingspan:* 49'6"
(15.09 m)   *Cruising speed:* 206 mph (331 km/h)

Very rare. These are similar, but the model 10 has five side windows; the model 12, three. *Twin radial engines on low-wing, classic double-fin Lockheed tail; tail plane extends through the fin; main landing gear quite visible when retracted into open wheel wells.*

The model 10, first flown in 1934, was America's first all-metal-skin airplane. Quickly adopted by airlines, it carried 12 passengers and a crew of two. The smaller "Electra, Jr." model 12, carrying six passengers and a crew of two, was intended for the corporate plane and feeder airline business. Though only a couple of dozen 12s and not more than 5 model 10s are flying, we could not exclude these grandparents of a famous family of propeller airliners, culminating in the Super Constellation.

Lockheed L18 Lodestar, C-60, PV-1, PV-2

Length: 49'10" (15.37 m)   *Wingspan:* 65'6" (20.21 m)   *Cruising speed:* 229 mph (368 km/h)

Rare and worth looking for. *Wing mounted just below midpoint of fuselage; twin tail; tail plane extends through tail fins; two radial engines.* The more common Beech 18 is much smaller, and does not have the Lockheed-type tail planes extending through the vertical fins.

The premier short-haul airliner just as World War II started and a common personnel carrier (C-60) through the war. A distinctly tail-dragging aircraft with the nose pointed up as if it should be flying, it's usually seen sitting idle on a runway apron. Carried 14 passengers in relative comfort, including a full lavatory in the rear of the aircraft. PV-1, PV-2 were early WWII long-range patrol bombers.

Cessna Bobcat, Crane, T-50, AT-8, C-78

Length: 32'9" (10 m)   *Wingspan:* 41'11" (12.8 m)   *Cruising speed:* 165 mph (265 km/h)

Rare, small, and old-fashioned-looking twin, with *huge radials compared to the size of the plane; long-nosed, but the nose barely extends past the engine nacelles; partially retractable landing gear.*

Built by the thousands from 1940 to 1945 as a primary (T-50) and advanced (AT-8) multiengine trainer for the U.S. (Bobcat) and Canadian (Crane) armed forces. Several hundred served as light transports (C-78). Many converted to civil air after WII, but wooden wings did not allow conversion to more efficient turboprops. Slightly underpowered, they're not really flyable on one engine; nevertheless, a durable, reliable short-haul aircraft.

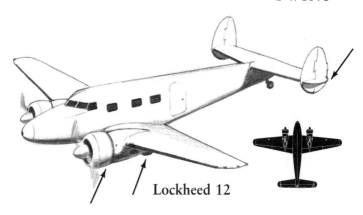

Lockheed 12

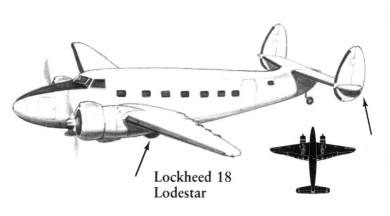

Lockheed 18
Lodestar

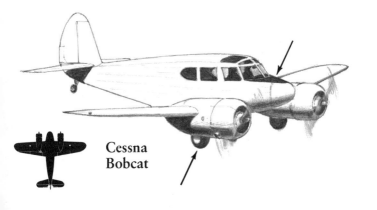

Cessna
Bobcat

North American B-25 Mitchell

Length: 52'11" (16.33 m)   *Wingspan:* 67'7" (20.86 m)   *Cruising speed:* 250 mph (402 km/h)

Rare, variable. Combines *midwing with double tail fins.* Note that it is a "high" midwing, and the tail plane does not extend through the vertical fins. Compare the somewhat similar Lockheed Lodestar, with its much lower wing mounting and tail plane extending through the twin tail fins.

Designed before World War II, more than 10,000 were built; losses kept the inventory to about 2600 maximum during WWII. Produced with and without the glass bombardier's nose; civil conversions usually have closed-in noses and some will have tip-tanks; a few have passenger windows. Once fairly popular as an aerial sprayer. Carrier-launched B-25s made the token attack on Tokyo in April 1942; B-25s were the aircraft seen in the 1970s movie *Catch-22.*

Douglas A-26 Invader

Length: 53'10" (16.40 m)   *Wingspan:* 70' (21.34 m)   *Cruising speed:* 325 mph (523 km/h)

Rare, variable. Look for the constants. *Wing mounted very high, but not above fuselage; two huge, cylindrical engine nacelles that extend well forward and back of the wing; nacelles mounted low on wing; long bulging nose; shallow cockpit windows.*

Once you get the configuration, you can ignore the dozens of variations of the basic aircraft: As a high-speed, large-capacity executive conversion, you may run across A-26s with completely enclosed noses, with passenger windows, and with tip-tanks on the wings, but the basic wing and engine conformation is undisturbed and unmistakable. Known as the A-26 (for attack bomber) through WWII, but redesignated B-26 after the war. The WWII B-26 was the Martin Marauder, with short, tapering engine nacelles.

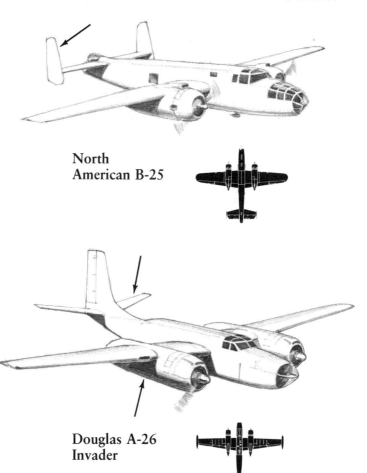

North
American B-25

Douglas A-26
Invader

de Havilland DHC7 Dash 7

Length: 80'8" (24.58 m)   *Wingspan:* 93' (28.35 m)   *Cruising speed:* 235 mph (378 km/h) Mach 0.354

Common. The only *four-engine, high-wing, T-tail* commercial aircraft in North America. Even when seen directly overhead, when it might be confused with the high-wing, conventional-tail C-130 Hercules, it is much slimmer and combines *four engines with nacelles that do not show behind the wing with a symmetrical taper on both edges of the wing from the fuselage to the wing tip.*

A popular short-haul airliner, this Canadian import can carry 50 passengers from rural airports with very short runways. A few windowless models are used for air-freight operations, mostly in the Canadian back country. The Canadian Coast Guard flies a marine reconnaissance type (the DHC-7R Ranger) with bubble observer windows on the lower part of the fuselage and a belly-bulge radar dome.

Lockheed Constellation (C-69, C-121)

L1049 Super Constellation specifications: *Length:* 116'2" (35.41 m) *Wingspan:* 123' (37.5 m)   *Cruising speed:* 260 mph (418 km/h)

Rare, almost none still flying. A very large *four-engine, low-wing* airliner/air-cargo hauler with *triple tail fins; tail plane extends through outboard fins.*

Once the queen of the transoceanic airways, a few Connies rest on runway aprons between charter flights. Most common was the L1049, carrying up to 110 passengers, built from 1943 to 1958. A few were converted to radar planes, designated EC-121, USAF, and Navy. These had top and bottom radar bulges at the wing area of the fuselage. The rarest is the last model, the L1649, with a wing design similar to the Electra/Orion's, a straight leading edge perpendicular to the centerline of the fuselage.

Vickers Viscount 700

Length: 81'2" (24.75 m)   *Wingspan:* 94' (28.66 m)   *Cruising speed:* 315 mph (507 km/h)

A large, four-turboprop airliner with *rather large oval passenger windows: bumpy cockpit with an odd, shouldered effect (see the de Havilland Heron, page 142, for a similar treatment); very long, slim engine nacelles; three-piece cockpit side windows; slight dihedral in wing; sharp dihedral in tail plane.*

First prototype flown in 1948; first production 700 in 1952, carrying 40 to 59 passengers, depending on seating chosen. There is an even rarer type 800, with a stretched fuselage and 13 passenger windows, which carries up to 71 passengers. Originally named the Viceroy, after the title of the British ruler of India; renamed the Viscount after Indian independence. The world's first turboprop airliner, the Viscount managed to penetrate the American market briefly in the late 1950s.

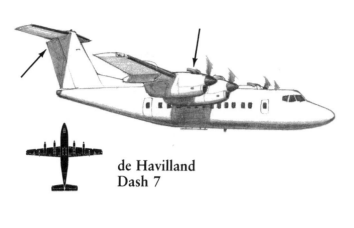

de Havilland
Dash 7

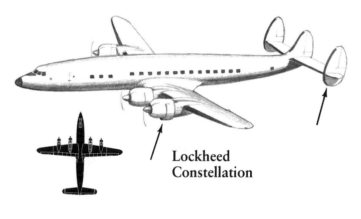

Lockheed
Constellation

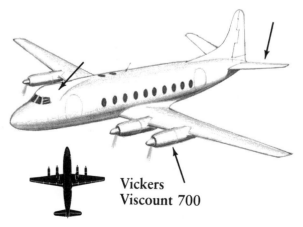

Vickers
Viscount 700

de Havilland Heron

Length: 48'6" (14.8 m)   *Wingspan:* 71'6" (21.8 m)   *Cruising speed:* 285 mph (459 km/h)

Very rare. Except for the *bulging bump over the cockpit,* a wonderfully symmetrical plane. *Slight dihedral in wings and tail planes;* overhead, *symmetrically tapering wing and tail surfaces.*

Popular airframes are hard to kill: The twin-engine British transport Dove was scaled up and given four engines to become the Heron. Several private companies have put turboprop engines on Herons, the most common a Riley Turbo Skyliner. Except as executive planes, you are most likely to encounter the few remaining Herons in the Caribbean. Note the classic British touch: Engines are centered vertically on the wing.

Douglas DC4, DC6, and DC7

(Old military designations: The DC4 was the C-54 Skymaster; the DC6 was the C-118 Liftmaster)
Lengths: (DC4, DC6) 93'11" (28.6 m); (DC6A and DC6B) 110'7" (30.66 m); (DC7) 112'3" (34.21 m)   *Wingspans:* (DC4, DC6, and DC7B) 117'6" (35.8 m); DC7C 127'6" (38.86 m)   *Cruising speeds:* (DC4) 227 mph (365 km/h); (DC6) 313 mph (504 km/h); (DC-7) 310 mph (499 km/h)

Once you've positively identified one of the DC series, picking the specific one is a matter of size: *The only conventional-tail planes with four radial engines* in *nacelles that do not extend behind the wing's trailing edge.* (Constellation, previous page, has similar engine nacelles.) *DC4s have round windows; others are square.*

Now scarce as hen's teeth, the DC series, beginning with the pre–WWII DC4, once dominated American aviation. All powered with radial piston engines, they became increasingly uneconomical in the face of new and sophisticated turboprop aircraft and did not survive well into the jet age. As military C-54 Skymasters, they ferried troops through the Korean War era. For the few remaining, separate them from other four-engine propeller jobs by the clearly radial piston engines. (Electras and CL-44s are turboprops, with slim, forward-extending engine housings; Herons have in-line piston engines that resemble four Spitfire or Mustang noses mounted on the wings, or they have been converted to turboprops.) The unstretched DC6 has no passenger windows forward of the wing; the DC6A and DC6B have two windows ahead of the wing; DC7s have three forward windows. The last and largest of the series, the DC7C, has the wingspan increased by 5 feet on each side by the insertion of a rectangular 5-foot wing root at the fuselage, a good mark when the craft is directly overhead. In general, overhead, the DC4, DC6, and DC7 series is marked by the engines showing only forward of the leading edge and by the symmetrically tapering tail planes — the DC4 tail plane is rounded, much like an old Piper Cub's. (An Electra's leading wing edges make a straight line at right angles to the fuselage, and the tail plane edges are not symmetrical. Similar four-engine prop jobs show some nacelle behind the wing.)

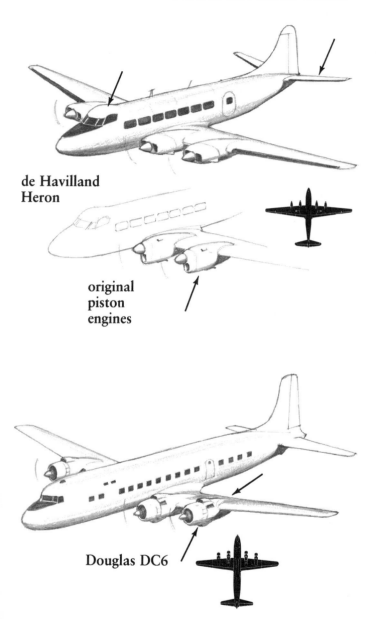

de Havilland
Heron

original
piston
engines

Douglas DC6

Lockheed L188 Electra

Length: 104'6" (31.8 m)   *Wingspan:* 99' (30.18 m)   *Cruising speed:* 405 mph (652 km/h)

Rare. Large, *low wing,* with *four turboprops; leading edge of wing straight and at right angles to fuselage; conventional tail.* Military reconnaissance version, P-3 Orion in limited use.

The jet-prop Electra came into service in 1959, just before the jet age, and in its first 18 months, its image was tarnished by two fatal crashes due to structural problems in the wing. Buyer resistance lasted until the small, true jet airliners had grabbed the commercial market. But the refitted Electras remain in service today as feeder airliners and especially as cargo planes. Like the newer CL44 and Dash 7, the turboprop Electra is much more fuel-efficient than jet aircraft, and it operates at nearly 80 percent of jet speeds. There is one possible confusion: Directly overhead, the plane resembles Lockheed's military C-130 Hercules, since you may not see that the C-130 has a high wing and an upswept rear fuselage. Note the difference in the nose shapes of the C-130 and the L188. (See Lockheed P-3 Orion, in military section, page 174.)

Canadair CL44

Length: 151'10" (46.28 m)   *Wingspan:* 142'3" (43.37 m)   *Cruising speed:* 380 mph (611 km/h)

Four turboprops on midwings and *ring around the tail* where the fuselage swings open; *fuselage hinged on port side; cockpit windows extend to top of fuselage:* Compare with low-wing, radial-engine DC4 series; overhead, *slim turboprop engine nacelles extend far forward of the wing's leading edge.*

The CL44 is a fuel-efficient, long-range cargo plane, with a very few passenger versions in service in Canada. Except for the massive tail fin, it looks very conventional. First flown in 1959. The hinge area forward of the tail is usually painted a color different from the rest of the fuselage. Developed from the British Britannia, as the CC-106 transport for the Canadian armed forces; then, with the swing tail, developed into the civilian CL44. CL44s are not uncommon at East Coast airports, where they haul freight on the North Atlantic routes.

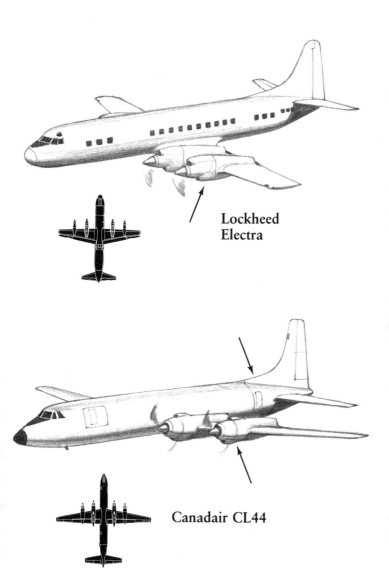

Lockheed
Electra

Canadair CL44

Avtek 400A

Length: 39'4" (11.99 m)   *Wingspan:* 35' (10.67 m)   *Forewing span:* 22'8" (6.92 m) *Cruising speed:* 419 mph (675 km/h)

Prototypes only, at time of publication: *Long thin forewing sits above and behind cockpit,* this to improve pilot's visibility compared to typical "canard" designs (see next two entries).

This child of the 1980s should finally see production in the 1990s. Design inspired by Al Mooney, the early designer of hot conventional aircraft. The standard turboprop engine is mounted upside down and backwards (on top of wing and pushing), which makes sense: It gets the air intake in front of the exhaust, where it belongs. Plane is a flying testbed for DuPont fibers imbedded in Dow resins, and this composite construction has provided most of the development funding.

Piaggio P180 Avanti

Length: 46'6" (14.17 m)   *Wingspan:* 45'5" (13.84 m)   *Forewing span:* 10'9" (3.28 m)   *Cruising speed:* 368 mph (593 km/h)

If it weren't for the *short canard wing under the cockpit* and the *upside down and backwards pushing turboprop engines,* this T-tailed metal-skinned aircraft would look fairly conventional.

This is a tweaked-up airplane, using a standard Piaggio wing design but inserting it into the middle of the rear end of the fuselage, taking popular turboprop engines but reversing them to pushers, and taking metal skin but shaping it in large sections and conforming the interior structure to the skin, the reverse of normal manufacturing. In the air, with its way-back wing, it looks as if the fuselage is dragging the rest of the plane along behind it.

Beech Starship I

Length: 46'1" (14.04 m)   *Wingspan:* 54'5" (16.60 m)   *Forewing span, extended:* 25'6" (7.79 m)   *Cruising speed:* 340 mph (546 km/h)

With its *tall* (8'1", 2.45 m) *winglets on a swept-back rear-mounted wing* and its *low, variable-angle forewing* and factory-delivered *pure white paint job,* this pusher-prop is highly noticeable.

This is the first of the new generation pusher-props to be delivered to customers. Although few in number, Starships have been seen across the U.S. and Canada. Still rare, but *visually obvious and unforgettable,* like a bald eagle.

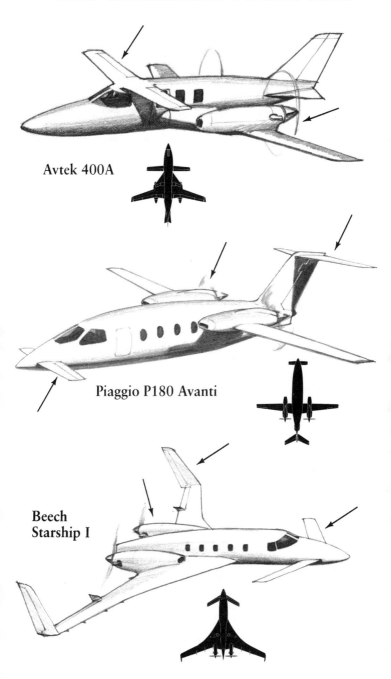

NEW GENERATION PUSHER-PROP

Avtek 400A

Piaggio P180 Avanti

Beech
Starship I

Learjet 23, 24D

Model 24D specifications: *Length:* 43'3" (12.5 m)   *Wingspan:* 35'7" (10.84 m)   *Cruising speed:* 481 mph (774 km/h)

The original small Learjet. *Fuselage-mounted twin jets reach over the wing's trailing edge; tip-tanks; wings with straight trailing edge; evenly tapered swept leading edge.*

The four-passenger Learjet 23 and the six-passenger Learjet 24 are usually distinguished by the number of windows and the tail configuration. The 23 will show two passenger windows on the right side and one on the left behind the passenger door. Most 24s show three passenger windows on the right, two on the left. Model 23s have a bullet at the center of the tail plane; most 24s do not.

Gates Learjet 25D, 28, 29

Length: 47'7" (14.50 m)   *Wingspan:* 35'7" (10.85 m)   *Cruising speed:* 528 mph (850 km/h)

One of a family of similar Learjets. The 25 series has *five windows on the right and four on the left behind the passenger door; wings have straight trailing edge; leading edge sweeps evenly* (compare the Learjet 35 or 36); *T-tail.*

The eight-passenger 25 is the stretched version of the successful Learjet series 23/24. In a quick glance, it could be confused with the larger Learjet 35 or 36, but note the 2-foot-long equal-chord wing extension and the much larger engines on the 35 and 36. Models 28, 29 use the Longhorn wing.

Learjet 35A, 36A, 31A

Length: 48'8" (14.8 m)   *Wingspan:* 39'6" (12 m)   *Cruising speed:* 529 mph (851 km/h)

Like the Learjet 25, but with *large turbofan engines that extend above the top of the fuselage;* wings lengthened by a *2-foot equal-chord extension at the wing tip; five windows on the right, four on the left.*

Introduced in 1973. Increased wingspan and larger engines make the 35 (eight-passenger) and 36 (luxury seating for four) capable of nonstop transcontinental or intercontinental range. Newest in the "30" series is the 31A, with the Longhorn wing.

Learjet Longhorn 55, 60

Length: 55'1" (16.79 m)   *Wingspan:* 43'9" (13.34 m)   *Cruising speed:* 523 mph (842 km/h)

Fuselage bulky forward, slim aft; characteristic *upturned winglets* at wing tips; six rectangular windows right side, four on left behind passenger door; compare with the much larger Gulfstream III (page 156). Gulfstream has five oval windows on each side and a more symmetrical fuselage. Note the Longhorn's sweeping two-piece windshield compared to the numerous smaller sections in the Gulfstream III. Model 60 is a 43" (1.1 m) stretch with an additional window on each side.

With seating for six to eight and 5 feet 8 inches of headroom, the Longhorn (first delivered in 1981) was Lear's entry into the medium-sized executive jet market.

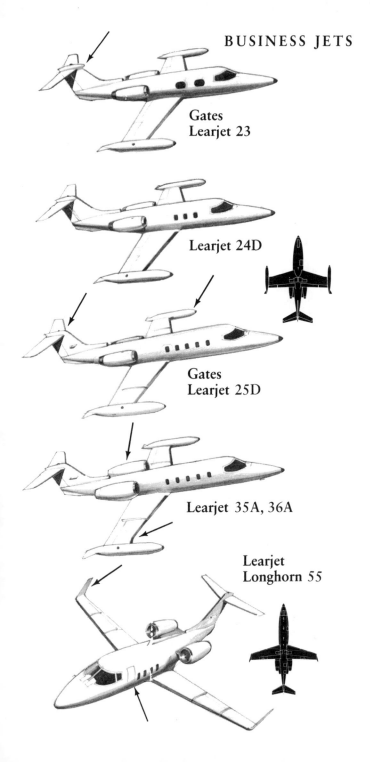

BUSINESS JETS

Gates
Learjet 23

Learjet 24D

Gates
Learjet 25D

Learjet 35A, 36A

Learjet
Longhorn 55

Cessna Citation I, II, SII, V, Citationjet

Citation I specifications: *Length:* 43'6" (13.26 m)   *Wingspan:* 47'1" (14.35 m)   *Cruising speed:* 420 mph (675 km/h)

A family of conventional-looking *twin fuselage-mounted jet* business aircraft; *unswept low tail plane, unswept wings tapering symmetrically.*

The first Cessna was the Fanjet 500, introduced in 1969. Citation I featured increased wingspan; Citation II is a stretch with 5 feet (1.52 m) more length and wingspan, and six windows instead of four. The high-performance SII has leading-edge extension at the wing root for more lift. The Citation V has the SII wing, stretches 2 feet (0.61 m), and adds a window, for a total of seven. The Citationjet, similar to the old Citation I, is an economy version for the less affluent.

Israel Aircraft Industries 1123 Westwind, Commodore, Jet Commander

Length: 52'3" (15.93 m)   *Wingspan:* 44'9" (13.65 m)   *Cruising speed:* 420 mph (676 km/h)

Fuselage-mounted twin jets; conventional tail; wing tip-tanks. (The only other planes with *factory tip-tanks* and twin fuselage-mounted jets are the Learjets, which have T-tails.) High overhead, you can separate these from Learjets by the gap between the wing trailing edge and the engine nacelle (the forward half of the Learjet engines rides up over the wings). The last model, the Westwind II, had winglets on the tip-tanks.

A ten-passenger jet designed in 1963. The design was sold to Israel Aircraft after the merger of Rockwell and North American in 1967. Part of the merger agreement required the combined firms to manufacture only one executive jet, and it kept the North American Sabreliner (page 152).

Israel Aircraft Industries 1125 Astra

Length: 52'9" (16.08 m)   *Wingspan:* 52'8" (16.05 m)   *Cruising speed:* 535 mph (862 km/h)

Compare with Dassault Falcon 200 and Rockwell Sabreliner (page 152) before deciding: *Low swept wing; horizontal stabilizer mounted low, but within the tail fin; long nose.* Falcon tail plane/horizontal stabilizer sits midway up the tail fin; Sabreliner's tail plane arises in the fuselage itself.

This is Israel's latest entry in the business jet market. The low wing increases cabin room, compared to the old IAI Westwind (above), with its inserted midwing; however, as with many "executive" jets, it helps to be under 5'6" (1.68 m) tall. As with other newer business jets, the Astra's quieter turbofan engines make it a better neighbor for those of us who live in an airport's sonic footprint.

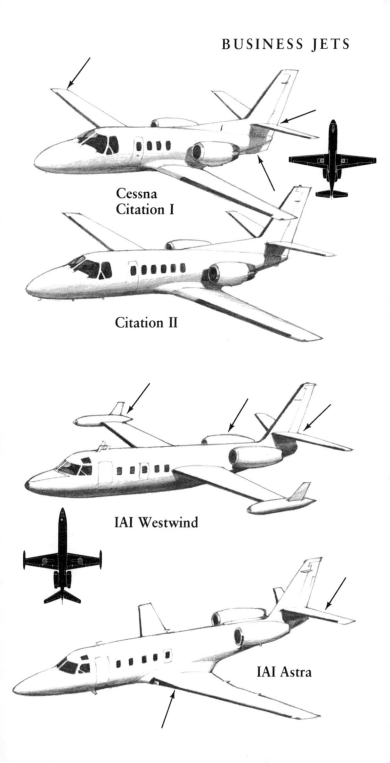

BUSINESS JETS

Cessna
Citation I

Citation II

IAI Westwind

IAI Astra

North American Rockwell Sabreliner, CT-39

Model 75 specifications: *Length:* 47'2" (14.38 m) *Wingspan:* 44'8"
(13.61 m) *Cruising speed:* 600 mph (965 km/h)

A series of very similar aircraft with slight dimensional changes.
Twin fuselage-mounted jets; conventional tail; fully swept wings (the
Cessna Citation I and II have straight wings and conventional tail;
the Falcon has swept wings with tail planes mounted midway up the
fin); *very chubby* compared to similarly sized exec-jets, giving 6 feet
of headroom inside.

Developed in 1958 as a utility and jet trainer for the military (supplied as T-39 and CT-39 to the USAF and the Navy), the military
Sabreliners and the old model 40 had three triangular windows behind the passenger door. Later stretched versions have five triangular
or square windows. The general appearance of the plane remained
unchanged by modifications. Accommodates 8 to 12 passengers,
depending on seating density.

Dassault Falcon 10, 100, 20, 200, HU-25, CC-117

Model 20 specifications: *Length:* 56'3" (17.15 m) *Wingspan:* 53'6"
(16.29 m) *Cruising speed:* 536 mph (862 km/h)

One of two fuselage-mounted twin jets with the *tail plane midway
up the tail fin* (compare the BAe 125, next page). *Falcon tail fin has a
very short fairing; strongly swept wings and tail plane.*

Popular as an executive, airline, and air-cargo plane, the Falcon 20
is being used by the U.S. Coast Guard (HU-25) and Canadian armed
forces (CC-117) as a long-range patrol plane. Various passenger and
cockpit window configurations, including the solid-bodied cargo
craft seen at so many U.S. airports. Model 10s and 100s are 11 feet
shorter in wingspan and length, with either three windows (model
10) or three port and four starboard (model 100). The Falcon 200 is
a modified 20, and was introduced in 1984.

Dassault Falcon 50, 500, 900

Length: 60' (18.29 m) *Wingspan:* 61'10" (18.86 m) *Cruising
speed:* 520 mph (837 km/h)

The only business-sized jet with *three engines, one mounted through
tail fin. A miniature L1011; tail plane mounted midway up tail fin.*

Certified in 1979, the Falcon 50 is an intercontinental business and
executive jet that takes the Falcon 20 airframe, adds a redesigned
wing, and substitutes three smaller turbofans for the two large ones
powering the 20. Used by the French government for VIP transportation. More than 100 sold to U.S. businesses. Carries eight passengers
in extreme comfort, with a range of more than 4000 miles (6500 km).
A Falcon 900 is a stretched 50, with 12 windows on each side.

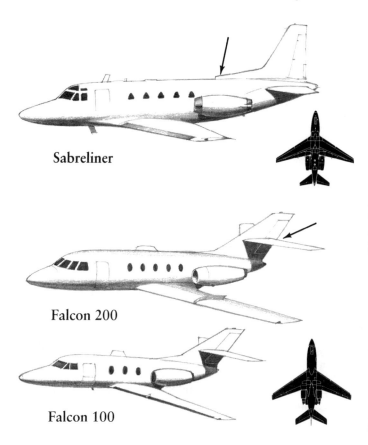

Sabreliner

Falcon 200

Falcon 100

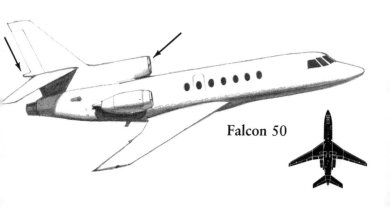

Falcon 50

Lockheed Jetstar, C-140

Length: 60'5" (18.42 m)   *Wingspan:* 54'5" (16.60 m)   *Cruising speed:* 508 mph (817 km/h)

Uncommon, unmistakable. Combines *four rear-mounted engines* with *massive fuel tanks "glove mounted" on wings.*

Lockheed's partly civil, partly military light transport was produced in small numbers, including 16 Jetstar I's for the U.S. Air Force (they have slightly smaller engines than illustrated). North American's Sabreliner (page 152) got most of the military business, and Lockheed stopped building Jetstars in 1981, after 21 years of production. Crew of two; ten passengers. Complete airliner appointments, including automatic oxygen mask delivery in case of loss of pressure. A few Jetstars have been converted to twin fan-jets, but fuel tanks are diagnostic.

British Aerospace 125, C-29

Length: 700, 50'8" (15.46 m)   *Wingspan:* 47' (14.33 m)   *Cruising speed:* 449 mph (722 km/h)

One of two aircraft with fuselage-mounted twin engines and *midway tail plane* (not T-tail); compare Dassault Falcon 20 (page 152). The 125 has *moderately swept wings* (the Falcon has a strong 30-degree sweep), and the 125 shows a *noticeable tail fin fairing rising out of the fuselage over the engines and a ventral fin below the tail* (the Falcon does not). The current model 700 has six windows, right side; the older model 125 has five.

A popular business jet; more than 600 of the 125 series sold from 1965 to 1980. Stretched and streamlined model 700 carries as many as 14 passengers. When marketed in the U.S. by Beech, it was known as the Beech Hawker. The refined model 800 was introduced in 1984.

Beechjet 400A, Mitsubishi Diamond

Length: 48'5" (14.75 m)   *Wingspan:* 43'6" (13.25 m)   *Cruising speed:* 515 mph (828 km/h)

Smallest of the *true T-tailed, swept-wing, twin fuselage-mounted jets without tip-tanks;* compare the bulkier (higher headroom) Canadair Challenger (page 156). The Beechjet has *six oval passenger windows that begin just behind the cockpit, including one in the passenger door.* The larger Canadair Challenger has six rectangular windows that begin behind the starboard-side passenger door.

Beechcraft acquired world manufacturing and sales rights (outside Japan) from Mitsubishi in 1985. The Japanese design, so similar to the Canadair, is yet another example of the convergent evolution of airplane "invention." Beechcraft has tweaked-up performance, passenger room, and appointments in the U.S.-built version. A subtle difference is the Beechjet's shallow fairing from mid-fuselage into the tail fin. The Challenger's vertical stabilizer arises abruptly from the fuselage.

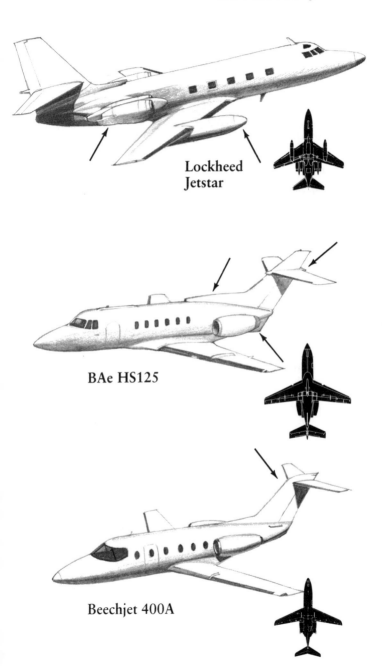

Lockheed
Jetstar

BAe HS125

Beechjet 400A

Cessna Citation III, VI, VII, X

Citation III specifications: *Length: 55'5"* (16.9 m)   *Wingspan: 53'4"* (16.24 m)   *Cruising speed:* 540 mph (869 km/h)

Separate this series from similar designs by the pleasingly *peculiar sculpted nose that flows into the wing roots, three non-trailing flap guides, "bullet" where the horizontal stabilizer crosses the tail fin, vertical TV-screen windows.*

A six- to ten-passenger luxury boss-hauler, certified to fly above the weather at more than 50,000 feet (15,240 m). The IV is a less luxurious entry-level model, the VII is a higher-performance III, and the X is a longer-range and slightly stretched version, showing six windows behind the portside doorway, seven on the right-hand side of the airplane.

Gulfstream II, III, IV

Gulfstream III specifications: *Length: 83'1"* (25.32 m)   *Wingspan: 77'10"* (23.72 m)   *Cruising speed:* 512 mph (824 km/h)

A *huge business jet* (two-thirds the size of an unstretched DC9); *shallow oval windows; T-tail, fuselage-mounted twin jets.* Accommodates eight passengers and a crew of three. Intercontinental range. Model II did not have winglets. The 1983 introduction, model IV, is 4'6" (1.37 m) longer and shows six, rather than five, passenger windows.

Grumman designed and built 258 Gulfstream IIs between 1967 and 1969. The U.S. Coast Guard operates one Gulfstream II as a VIP transport, clearly marked with the CG's red diagonal stripe. Don't confuse it with the Coast Guard Falcon 20 search planes, which have the tail plane mounted halfway up the fin and round windows.

Canadair 600 Challenger, 601, 601-3A, CL601 RJ

Canadair 600 specifications: *Length: 68'5"* (20.85 m)   *Wingspan: 61'10"* (18.85 m)   *Cruising speed:* 509 mph (819 km/h)

One of the largest and thickest of the *T-tailed business jets. Five visible, deep flap guides on each wing, and quite square windows.*

A series of jets, all airliner-deep through the fuselage, with headroom for six-foot-tall (1.83 m) passengers. The 601 has winglets and even larger turbofan engines, the 601-3A has eight windows and a luxury interior for 10 passengers. Newest is the 601 RJ (regional jet), stretched to 88'5" (26.95 m), which carries up to 50 passengers. It shows 13 windows on each side and is the size of the original DC9.

Cessna
Citation III

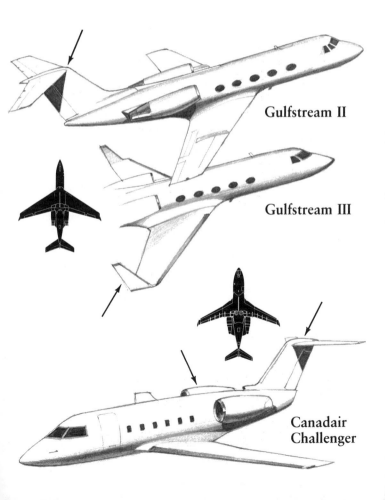

Gulfstream II

Gulfstream III

Canadair
Challenger

BAC 111 (One-Eleven)

Series 500 specifications: *Length:* 107' (32.61 m)   *Wingspan:* 93'6"
(28.5 m)   *Cruising speed:* 461 mph (742 km/h)

A *low-wing, T-tail, fuselage-mounted twin-jet* airliner. Note four
field marks separating it from the similar DC9 and Fokker Fellowship: combines *pointed nose, oval windows, three flap guides on
each wing that trail behind, distinct bullet on tail plane.*

Certified in 1965 as a 79-passenger series 200 aircraft, the most
common variant in the U.S. is the stretched series 500, carrying up to
119 passengers. Basically a short-haul aircraft, it is also produced in
a variant for small, high-altitude, hot-weather airports: the series
475 — 14 feet shorter, but with the long wings and high power of the
stretched 500. Now manufactured under license in Romania.

Fokker F28 Fellowship, 100

Model Mk4000 specifications: *Length:* 97'1" (29.61 m)   *Wingspan:*
82'3" (25.07 m)   *Cruising speed:* 421 mph (677 km/h)

Quite rare in the U.S. A *stubby, low-wing, T-tail, fuselage-
mounted, twin-jet* airliner. Separate from the much more common
DC9 or BAC111 by these marks: *short, rounded nose; oval windows; distinct fairing from fuselage to tail fin; two flap guides on
each wing that trail behind; squared-off rear fuselage housing a clam-
shell airbrake.*

Fokker attempted to cut out a particular market segment with this
short-haul, high-performance aircraft. Carrying a maximum of 85
passengers in the Mk4000 configuration, the Fellowship is highly
fuel-efficient and suitable for intercity hops of as little as 30 minutes'
flying time. A stretched model 100 carries 97 to 122 and has been
ordered by American Airlines.

McDonnell Douglas DC9, MD80 to MD90

MD80 specifications: *Length:* 147'10" (45.06 m)   *Wingspan:*
107'10" (32.87 m)   *Cruising speed:* 565 mph (909 km/h)

Ninety-nine times out of a hundred, if you see a medium-length to
very long airliner with two rear-mounted engines, it will be one version or another of the DC9, MD80 to MD90 aircraft. They range
from old 50-passenger models to stretched MD90s that carry 158
passengers. To separate out the ones that are similar in size to the
BAC One-Eleven, note the absence of a bullet where the tail plane
crosses the tail fin, and note the flap guides that do *not* extend past
the wing's trailing edge. The rare Fokker Fellowship has a much stubbier nose, two trailing flap guides, and a curious squared-off tail. The
old DC9s were the noisiest twin-engine jets of their generation. With
the new fan-jets and redesigned wings, the MDs are among the quiet-
est of airliners.

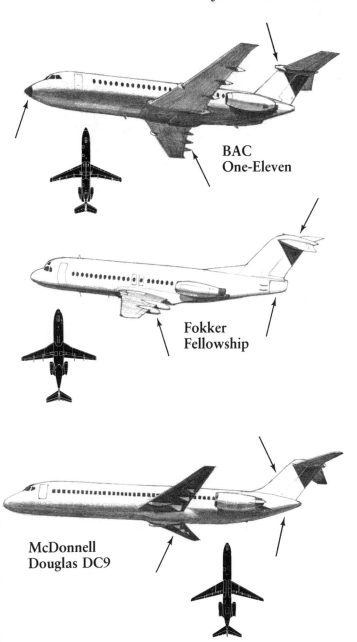

BAC
One-Eleven

Fokker
Fellowship

McDonnell
Douglas DC9

Boeing 727

Length: 153'2" (46.69 m)   *Wingspan:* 108' (32.92 m)   *Cruising speed:* 570 mph (917 km/h)

The only airliner you'll see in North America with *three rear-mounted engines: one in the tail, the others on fuselage pods.* If someone should import a British Trident, it will have a distinct bullet at the center of the tail plane. The Russian military TU154 should not appear at all, but if seen elsewhere, note that it has a long pointed bullet at the tail plane.

First flown in 1963, the 727-100 (length, 133'2", 40.58 m) sold moderately to U.S. customers for medium-range flights. Since the introduction of the 727-200, which is 20 feet longer than the 727-100, Boeing has sold nearly 2000. As many as 189 passengers can fit, without much comfort, into a one-class 727-200, 90 more than the original 727-100.

McDonnell Douglas MD10 (DC10), KC-10 "Extender," MD11

MD10 specifications: *Length:* 182'1" (55.50 m)   *Wingspan:* 165'4" (50.41 m)   *Cruising speed:* 540 mph (869 km/h)

Common at all large airports. *A wide-body with two wing-mounted engines and a tail engine that blows straight through the tail fin, above the fuselage.* In military paint it's an Air Force in-flight refueling plane.

First of the tri-engines to carry passengers (1971), and built in a variety of performance models, mostly by changing engines rather than general configuration. A newer MD11 is 18 feet longer (200 feet overall, 60.96 m) and has 323 seats in the usual three classes. An MD12 is planned, with wingspan extended to 211 feet (64.31 m) and a length of 217 feet (66.14 m).

Lockheed L1011 TriStar

Length: 177'8" (54.17 m); Model 500, 165'8" (50.5 m)   *Wingspan:* 155'4" (47.35 m)   *Cruising speed:* 558 mph (898 km/h)

A *jumbo wide-body; two engines on wings; one rear-mounted at tail.* Separate from the DC10 by noting that the *tail-mounted engine has intake above the fuselage and exhausts through end of the fuselage.* Compare the DC10 tail engine, which carries straight through the tail fin.

A popular wide-body that has never suffered from a single serious mechanical defect, the L1011 was sold for only ten years, 1972–1982, before Lockheed withdrew from the passenger jet field, leaving it to Boeing and McDonnell Douglas, whose DC10 was a direct competitor to the L1011. Fewer than 300 are in service. The long-range model 500 is not noticeably shorter, but it can be picked out on the flight line by the way the tail engine is faired directly into the fuselage (see sketch above model drawing).

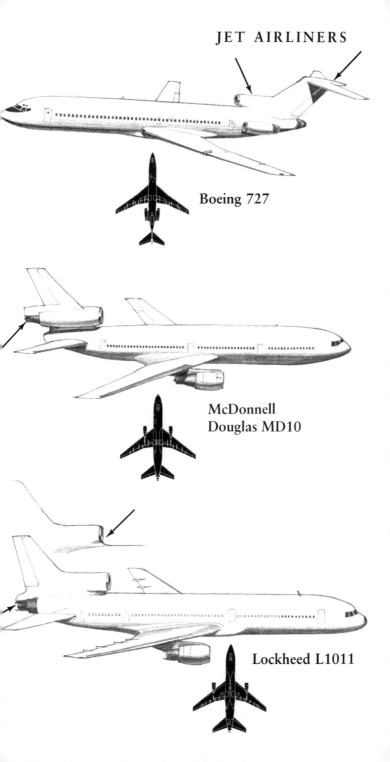

JET AIRLINERS

Boeing 727

McDonnell
Douglas MD10

Lockheed L1011

Boeing 737-200, -300, -400, -500

737-300 specifications: *Length:* 109'7" (33.40 m)   *Wingspan:* 94'9" (28.88 m)   *Cruising speed:* 564 mph (907 km/h)

Even when stretched a little (models 300, 400, 500), a *stubby twin underwing jet* that can, from a distance, appear to be a wide-body. The original 737-200 has *slim engine nacelles that extend equally in front of and behind the wing.* The 300, 400, 500 have large-diameter fan-jets mounted on pylons. Overhead, where relative size is hard to judge, they could be confused with Airbus A300s, or 767s. The 737 has three flap guides; the 767 has four almost invisible guides; the A300 has five noticeable guides.

The primary short-haul jet of the 1970s, it carried only 120 passengers then, and even the stretched (110 feet, 33.53 m) 400 carries only 146 today. It has excellent short-field qualities, and a number of 200s were modified for use on gravel airstrips in Africa, the Middle East, and Latin America.

Boeing 757

Length: 154'8" (47.14 m)   *Wingspan:* 124'6" (37.95 m)   *Cruising speed:* 494 mph (795 km/h)

Slim-bodied, with *two large turbofans* mounted under the wing, *showing well forward* of the wing. This plane should separate easily from the wide-bodied, twin-turbofan airplanes, but compare it to the Airbus A-300 and the Boeing 737 and 767. The combination of normal fuselage and engines is diagnostic.

From the passenger's point of view, the 757 is nothing more than a stretched, re-engined version of Boeing's popular 727 aircraft. Other differences are subtle, but include a wing with less sweepback and greater depth (chord). The 757 is 19 feet longer than the 727. Like the stretched DC9, the 757 carries more passengers and is certified to fly with two, rather than three, flight officers — a considerable saving.

Airbus A320

Length: 123'3" (37.57 m)   *Wingspan:* 111'3" (33.91 m)   *Cruising speed:* 515 mph (829 km/h)

Not much bigger than a 737, but *a truly wide-bodied medium-length twin jet.* Like all the Airbuses, it has the *very noticeable flap guides.* The winglets are *wing fences, up-and-down winglets. Noticeable double-bubble cross section at wing root* for baggage and containers. Like other Airbuses, the top of the fuselage runs into the tail on a nearly straight line, giving the appearance of greater upsweep on the bottom of the fuselage. Boeings are tapered symmetrically, like ice cream cones.

Conventional enough on the outside, the Airbus A320 is highly advanced internally, with the first fly-by-wire controls in the subsonic industry operated with side-stick controllers (no control columns or wheels in the cockpit). It has wide aisles for easy passenger exiting (and thus quick turnarounds) and has wider and deeper seats than older airplanes of any manufacture.

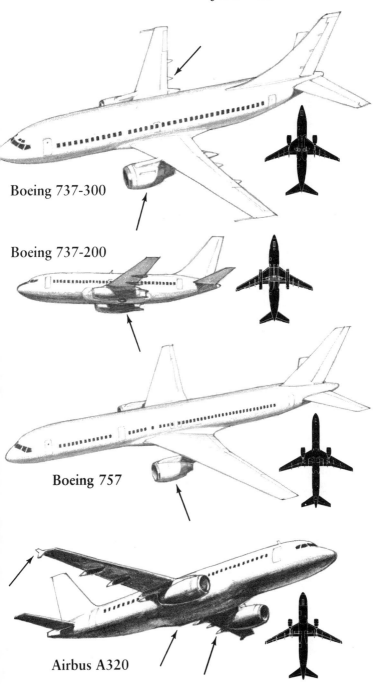

JET AIRLINERS

Boeing 737-300

Boeing 737-200

Boeing 757

Airbus A320

Airbus A300, A310

A300-600 specifications: *Length:* 177'5" (54.08 m)   *Wingspan:* 147'1" (44.84 m)   *Cruising speed:* 543 mph (875 km/h)

A pair of *wide-bodied, twin underwing-engined* airliners (the A310 is shorter by 24'4", 7.42 m), separated from their Boeing look-alikes by several marks: Airbuses have *large flap guides that trail behind the wing,* no *dihedral in tail plane, and a typical rear fuselage that extends straight back on the top, with all the taper taken up by the bottom, giving the illusion of an upturn in the tail section.* Latest models have little triangular "wing fences" (up-and-down winglets).

These remarkably similar aircraft are available in several subspecies, including longer-range (extra fuel tanks) and convertible, cargo-to-passenger, configurations. Like most new airliners, a highly computerized flight system allows certification with a crew of two.

Boeing 767-200, -300

767-200 specifications: *Length:* 159'2" (48.51 m)   *Wingspan:* 156'1" (47.57 m)   *Cruising speed:* 494 mph (795 km/h)

A pair of twin wing-mounted jet airliners (the 767-300 stretches to 180'3", 54.94 m), not too difficult to distinguish from the Airbuses: *Three barely noticeable flap guides* (not five obvious ones); *tail of fuselage tapers symmetrically beneath the tail fin; noticeable dihedral in tail planes.* A subtle difference, but clear when planes are on the ground: *Where the trailing edge of Boeing tail fin meets the fuselage, it is forward of the trailing control surfaces on the tail planes.*

The more than 20 models of 767s, including the obvious stretches and the ones with extra internal fuel tanks, can carry from 240 to 300 passengers and operate at ranges from 3708 miles (5967 km) to 7836 miles (12,611 km). That kind of doubling of performance, with gradations along the way, creates a plane for every airline's needs.

Boeing 777

Length: 209'1" (63.73 m)   *Wingspan:* 199'11" (960.93 m)
Estimated cruising speed: 494 mph (795 km/h)

Expected to fly in 1994, this will be the jumboest of the twin-engine jumbos. On the ground, it can be distinguished from the 767s by sheer size and by the two passenger doors in front of the wing (767-300s have an escape door *over* the wing). *Bulky fairings at the wing roots somewhat resemble Airbus configuration.*

The 777 will fill the gap between the stretch 767-300 and the new, massive 747-400, in both number of passengers and range. The planned long-range 777 can take 313 passengers in the typical three classes (the 747-400 hauls 386 in three classes) and fly them from London to Los Angeles nonstop.

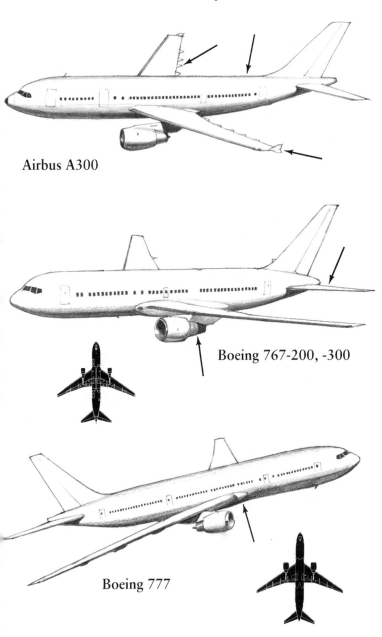

JET AIRLINERS

Airbus A300

Boeing 767-200, -300

Boeing 777

British Aerospace BAe146-100, 200, 300

Length: 93'8" (28.55 m) *Wingspan:* 86'5" (26.34 m) *Cruising speed:* 440 mph (708 km/h)

New in 1982. Smallest of the four-engined jets; *massive fin to T-tail* (not unlike de Havilland's Dash turboprops); *large flap tracks underwing — bulging landing gear fairings on belly;* the only four-jet-on-the-wing T-tail.

Designed over several years, beginning in 1973, by the ailing British aerospace industry, the BAe146 is a short-haul jet that takes advantage of modern fan-jet engines to produce a quiet aircraft; it can land and take off in cities without annoying airport neighbors. First American purchase by Air Wisconsin.

McDonnell Douglas DC8

Series 60 specifications: *Length:* 187'5" (57.12 m) *Wingspan:* 148'5" (45.23 m) *Cruising speed:* 600 mph (965 km/h)

A series of *rare four-engine jet liners.* Compare with the Boeing 707-720 (next entry) before deciding. The most common variant is the extreme stretch Series 60: Viewed at any distance, it has the aspect of great fuselage length balanced on relatively negligible wings. On the ground, the tail fin has no vhf radio antenna (compare the 707 drawing); *smooth, cigar-shape engine nacelles; distinct "brow" at cockpit window; tail fin swept;* but *stretch 60 series even more radically swept.*

A popular airliner first flown in 1958. Most have been converted, whatever their original size, into the super stretches by the insertion of fuselage plugs fore and aft of the wings. Series 70 is a stretch with more efficient, quieter fan engines. Still flown, mostly as economy charters.

Boeing 707, 720

707-320 specifications: *Length:* 152'11" (46.61 m) *Wingspan:* 145'9" (44.42 m) *Cruising speed:* 550 mph (885 km/h)

The very rare 707 has a superficial resemblance to the Douglas DC8, but once you have identified the plane by some minor details, its configuration is quite different and instantly recognizable. *Four engines on wing, engine nacelles are distinctly larger forward* (compare the much smoother, cigarlike DC8 nacelles). *The engines are tucked up under the wing* (the DC8 engines carried a bit lower and a bit farther forward). *The cockpit windows are very close to the nose* (the DC8 has more nose to it).

The first U.S.-built jet liner, flown in 1954. Very successful; made in a number of variations for increased passenger capacity or for transoceanic flights. The similar 720 was a medium-range plane with thinner, slightly more swept wings and a distinct ventral fin. Alas, a few 707s (model 420) also carry the ventral fin. To muddle the issue further, American Airlines designated its 720s as 707-023s. The airframe is still built for military use as a long-distance radar platform and communication snooper and suppressor.

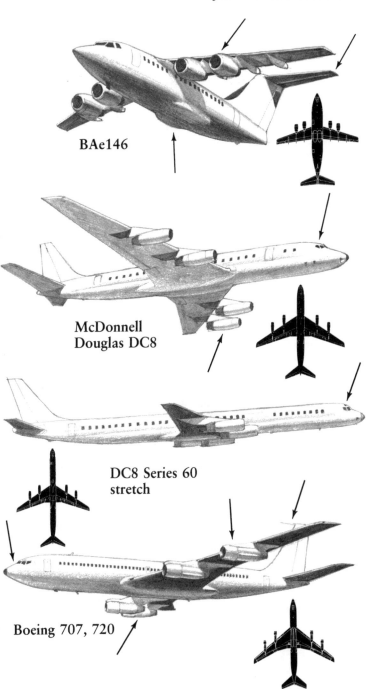

JET AIRLINERS

BAe146

McDonnell
Douglas DC8

DC8 Series 60
stretch

Boeing 707, 720

Boeing 747-200, 747SP, 747-300, 747-400

747-200 specifications: *Length:* 231'10" (70.66 m)   *Wingspan:* 195'8" (59.64 m)   *Cruising speed:* 604 mph (973 km/h)

Common and unmistakable, the *four-engine jumbo jet with the bulge behind the cockpit.* Variants are rarer, more challenging to identify: The stubby, long-range SP (47 feet, 14.33 m, shorter; bottom drawing), the stretched upper decks of the 300 (main drawing), and new 400 accommodate more passengers upstairs; and the 400 has winglets.

In 1992 the 747 will replace the old 707 as *Air Force One,* designated VC-25A. Additional 747s purchased by the Air Force from Pan American will be converted to long-range cargo haulers, designated C-19A, with a side cargo door. After conversion, the planes are returned to civilian service and held in reserve for emergency call-up. These new "military" 747s bring the plane full circle. The 747 was developed as an airliner from Boeing's unsuccessful entrant in the military wide-body transport competition won by the C-5A (page 188).

Airbus A340, A330

A340 specifications: *Length:* 194'10" (59.39 m)   *Wingspan:* 192'5" (58.65 m)   *Cruising speed:* 605 mph (974 km/h)

The A340 will be easy to identify. It will be the *giant four-engine jet that* doesn't bulge behind the cockpit. Unfortunately, the A330 will have an identical airframe with just two engines, right where the inboard engines are on an A340. Compare it to the similar Boeing 777: The A330 has *swept-back and out-canted winglets.* Like other Airbus designs, *the top of the fuselage carries a straight line from the cockpit to the tail fin;* compare to the conical Boeings.

Engineers took advantage of the Airbus configuration to build this competitor to the Boeing 747. The fuselage sections are nearly identical, as are the fly-by-wire controls. The 335-passenger A340-300 can compete over the Atlantic and throughout Europe; however, it has a considerably shorter range than the 747-300 — 5300 miles compared to the 747's 7020 (8525 km to 11,297 km).

Aerospatiale/BAC Concorde

Length: 203'9" (62.10 m)   *Wingspan:* 83'10" (25.55 m)   *Cruising speed:* 1336 mph (2150 km/h)

Rare, but seen frequently at Kennedy Airport and Miami. *Long, skinny fuselage with delta wings; four rectangular air intakes under wing; no tail planes at all.*

First flown in 1971; first passengers, 1975. After environmental complaints about sonic booms and upper-atmosphere air pollution, airport noise, and the quadrupling of the price of petroleum, the once-hopeful supersonic Concorde was dropped by every airline (more than 70 were on order at one time), except for the government-subsidized airlines of the manufacturing countries, British Airways and Air France. Can carry 128 passengers across the Atlantic in less than 3 hours.

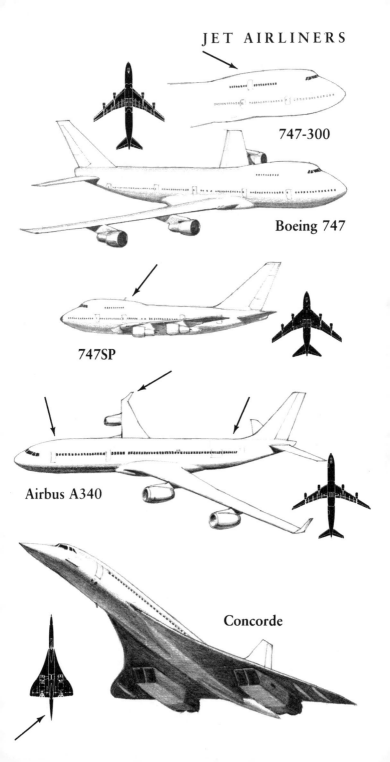

JET AIRLINERS

747-300

Boeing 747

747SP

Airbus A340

Concorde

Beech T-34C Mentor

Length: 28'8" (8.72 m)   *Wingspan:* 33'4" (10.16 m)   *Level flight:* 241 mph (388 km/h)

The Navy's only *slim-nosed, propeller-driven* airplane. *High green-house canopy; ventral fin; finlet fairings to tail plane; paired air-scoops; large side exhausts.*

The latest in a long line of Navy-style in-line trainers, including the SN-J (Texan) and the nonturbocharged Beech T-34 it replaces (page 48). The T-34C, with turboprop, is 90 mph faster than the T-34, making it an easier step up to the 343 mph T-28 Trojan used for carrier training (page 46). As with many trainers, it can be fitted with armaments and sold overseas for counterinsurgency missions.

Rockwell OV-10 Bronco

Length: 41'7" (12.67 m)   *Wingspan:* 40' (12.19 m)   *Cruising speed:* 210 mph (338 km/h)

Overhead, the *perfectly rectangular wing and tail plane* are diagnostic; on the ground, the twin booms to the tail extend naturally out of the engine nacelles. The Cessna Skymaster is the only remotely similar aircraft.

The little OV-10 is a short takeoff and landing observation and counterinsurgency aircraft that can operate without arresting gear from runways as short as the deck of a helicopter-carrying amphibious assault ship. A few heavily armed versions are in service with the U.S. Marines, including models for night observation: These have a distinctive probe extending from the nose that houses a forward-looking infrared sensor and laser used to guide missiles to the target. They are usually seen near bombing ranges, circling over practicing attack aircraft at a leisurely 55 mph.

Grumman OV-1 Mohawk

Length: 41' (12.5 m)   *Wingspan:* 48' (14.63 m)   *Level flight:* 289 mph (465 km/h)

Bulbous cockpit and *triple tail* give a sort of dragonfly look to the craft; *wing tanks* and a *right-side radar pod extend forward of nose.*

The Mohawk has such odd geometry that it can hardly be compared to any other aircraft. Though not all models have the curious radar pod that extends past the nose, the Grumman-style dihedral tail plane and triple tail fins are enough for positive identification. Most OV-1s carry two underwing fuel tanks just outboard of the engines. Only the Army flies the Mohawk, which is used as a target locater and battlefield mapper. The heavily armed Mohawks of the Vietnam War have been refitted, as the Air Force, Navy, and Marines captured the fixed-wing attack plane mission from Army aviation.

MILITARY AIRCRAFT

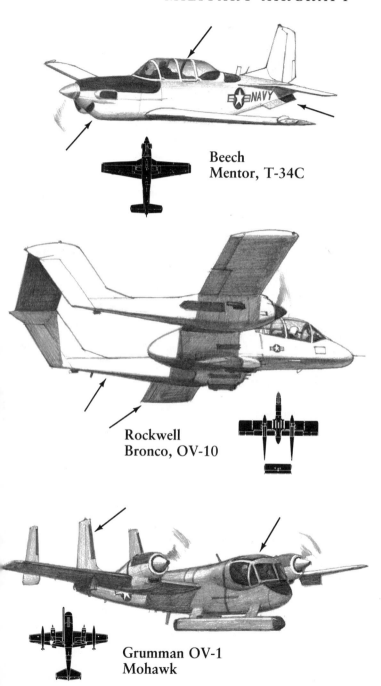

Beech
Mentor, T-34C

Rockwell
Bronco, OV-10

Grumman OV-1
Mohawk

Grumman E-2 Hawkeye and C-2 Greyhound

Length: 57'7" (17.6 m)   *Wingspan:* 80'7" (24.6 m)   *Cruising speed:* 296 mph (476 km/h)

The E-2 is an unmistakable *twin-engine* aircraft backpacking a *30-foot-diameter radar pancake.* The C-2 utility version is the *only high-wing twin prop with four tail fins.*

The Hawkeye's mission is early warning for the carrier fleet. The Greyhound serves as a shore-to-ship delivery system, carrying up to 39 passengers or 4 tons of freight. The type has certain Grumman characteristics, including a dihedral in the tail planes and engines that angle out slightly from the fuselage. (Note those features in Grumman's smaller OV-1, previous entry, which has three tail fins.) Overhead, it is the only twin-engine propeller aircraft that combines a straight trailing edge to the tail plane with symmetrically tapering wings.

Grumman S-2 Tracker, C-1 Trader and E-1 Tracer

Length: 43'6" (13.26 m)   *Wingspan:* 72'7" (22.13 m)   *Cruising speed:* 150 mph (241 km/h)

Increasingly rare. In service as the Trader only, a shore-to-ship cargo plane; *twin engines that extend fore and aft* of the *symmetrically tapering wings;* strong *dihedral in tail planes.*

A typical Grumman aircraft. Note the bug-eyed cockpit (see the Mohawk, previous page). When it was outfitted for advance warning of aircraft, it carried a teardrop-shaped radar dome 30 feet long (compare the current early-warning Hawkeye, with its round radar pod). Seen overhead, it could conceivably be confused with some commercial twin-engines, but the following combination is unique: symmetrically tapered wings; engine nacelles that extend well behind the wing; and a straight-line trailing edge on the tail plane.

de Havilland CC-115 Buffalo

Length: 79' (24.08 m)   *Wingspan:* 96' (29.26 m)   *Cruising speed:* 261 mph (420 km/h)

Fairly common military transport in Canada. *Combination of twin turboprop engines, upswept fuselage, and T-tail* is unique. There is a slight resemblance, at a distance, to the twin-engine Dash 8 commercial airliner.

The Buffalo is noticeably bulkier than the midtailed Caribou. The overhead view is much like the Caribou, the leading edge of the wing almost, but not quite, straight; the tail plane almost, but not quite, rectangular. In commercial service, it is designated DHC5; in Canadian armed forces, CC-115.

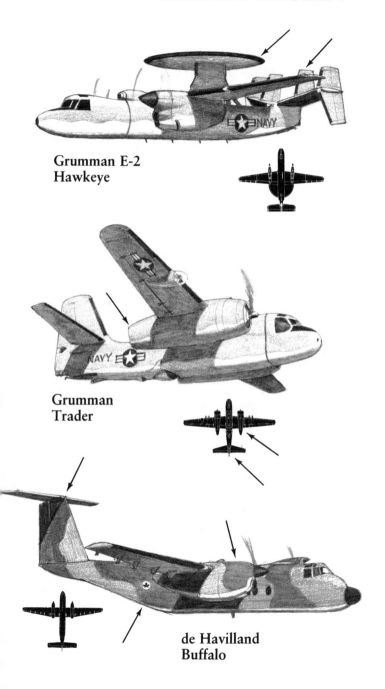

Grumman E-2
Hawkeye

Grumman
Trader

de Havilland
Buffalo

Lockheed C-130 Hercules

Length: 97'10" (29.78 m) *Wingspan:* 132'7" (40.41 m) *Cruising speed:* 340 mph (547 km/h)

Common, nationwide. *Combines upswept fuselage with an enormous conventional tail, radar dome nose,* and classic Lockheed wing; *straight leading edge at right angles to fuselage;* four turboprop engines.

The bulky C-130 bears no real resemblance, even overhead, to the more elegant and T-tailed de Havilland Dash 7 (page 140). (There is a Russian copy of the Hercules, the An-12 Cub.) Compare the overhead view of the Hercules with the Electra (page 144). The Hercules is bulkier, and its radar dome nose looks comical. The Orion's is simply the curved nose of the airplane. C-130s are operated by all four U.S. services in modes from gunships to weather observation and search and rescue, as well as transports. The C-130 was the type of aircraft used by the Israeli government on the successful mission to free the hijacked Air France passengers at Entebbe, Uganda, on July 3, 1976.

Lockheed P-3 Orion

Length: 116'10" (35.61 m) *Wingspan:* 99'8" (30.37 m) *Cruising speed:* 378 mph (608 km/h)

Unique but variable aircraft, seen worldwide. *Four long-nacelled propeller engines project well forward of the wings; engines are set well-out on relatively short wings; most models show the trailing magnetic detection boom* used in anti-submarine patrols. A few carry a round pancake radar dome above the wing; a few show neither magnetic boom nor radar dome, including NOAA weather planes based in Florida.

This is the old Lockheed Electra airliner, first converted to military use in 1959 and still in production after 42 years, flown by dozens of countries for coastal surveillance. Strong and durable, it routinely flies through hurricanes to gather weather data. A proposed successor, the P-7A, will look virtually identical to the P-3; although slightly longer (by 6'4", 1.93 m) and with considerable hidden changes in construction and weapons bays, it would clearly be an upgraded P-3 if it is built.

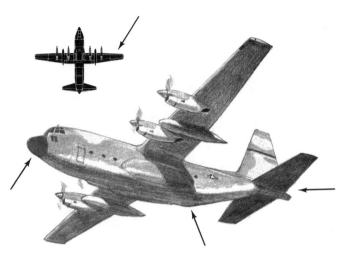

Lockheed C-130
Hercules

Lockheed P-3 Orion

Cessna A-37 Dragonfly and T-37

Length: 29′4″ (8.92 m)   *Wingspan:* 33′7″ (10.3 m)   *Level flight:* 507 mph (816 km/h) Mach 0.658 at sea level

Low straight wings with conspicuous tip-tanks and inconspicuous twin jets at the wing roots; bulbous cockpit for side-by-side seating in the trainer version. Nothing else flying has *twin wing-root jets and straight wings at right angles to the fuselage.*

Though many combat aircraft have been converted to trainers, the counterinsurgency A-37B was developed as a gunship from the USAF's standard jet trainer, the T-37. It saw wide use in areas of Vietnam not defended by surface-to-air missiles, carrying a 7.62 mm minigun capable of firing 6000 rounds a minute as well as cluster and phosphorus bombs. Suitable for use against lightly armed "insurgents," the A-37's low stall speed, under 100 mph, makes it a precision instrument.

Rockwell T-2 Buckeye

Length: 38′4″ (11.66 m)   *Wingspan:* 38′10″ (11.62 m)   *Level flight:* 522 mph (840 km/h) Mach 0.69 at sea level

Seen near naval flight schools and stateside aircraft carriers. *Large canopy* for tandem pilot and instructor; straight wings with tip-tanks; a *stubby, front-heavy look.*

The Navy's basic jet trainer used for teaching pilots to land on an aircraft carrier. It resembles the side-by-side seating USAF T-37 if the wing geometry is not visible. The T-2's engine intakes are well forward of the wing. First built as a single-engine trainer by North American, based on the Navy's retired FJ-1 Fury fighters. The twin version is all that flies today, and later models are the first Navy planes with fiber-glass wings. Rockwell also markets it as a counterinsurgency plane.

Fairchild A-10 Thunderbolt, "Warthog"

Length: 53′4″ (16.25 m)   *Wingspan:* 57′6″ (17.53 m)   *Level flight:* 443 mph (713 km/h) Mach 0.58 at sea level

Fuselage-mounted huge turbofan twin jets rise *above the fuselage;* overhead, note the *rectangular tail plane.*

The A-10 is a highly maneuverable ground support plane, essentially an aircraft wrapped around a 30 mm gun that fills the inside of the fuselage. The ammunition is typically simple cylinders of depleted (not radioactive) uranium that destroy tanks by mere impact. The A-10 is basically an alternative to smart bombs and heat-seeking missile systems, and relies heavily on the pilot, instead of sophisticated instrumentation, for success. Used heavily in the 1991 Gulf War against armor and Scud missile launchers.

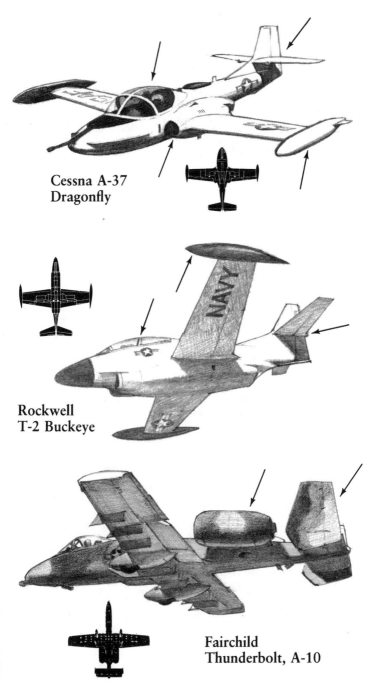

MILITARY AIRCRAFT

Cessna A-37
Dragonfly

Rockwell
T-2 Buckeye

Fairchild
Thunderbolt, A-10

BAe T-45 Goshawk

Length: 36'8" (11.17 m)   *Wingspan:* 30'10" (9.39 m)   *Level flight:*
Mach 0.85

A distinctive small jet seen near naval bases and aircraft carrier
ports: *Long, low bubble canopy covers tandem seating; noticeable
reversed dihedral in tail planes.* Up close, the carrier-landing modifications include a tail hook, ventral fin, and leading-edge slats on the
wings.

The original BAe Hawk was a British airstrip-based jet trainer,
now much modified as a U.S. Navy aircraft carrier trainer. The major
visible external change was the addition of leading-edge slats for better stall speeds and quicker rebounds from touch-and-go exercises (including inadvertent touch-and-go "bolter" landings). With numerous
modifications, it is the first land-based aircraft to be successfully converted to the complex task of flying on and off a moving carrier deck.

McDonnell Douglas A-4 Skyhawk

Length: 40' (12.2 m)   *Wingspan:* 27'6" (8.38 m)   *Level flight:*
675 mph (1086 km/h), Mach 0.89 at sea level

Almost extinct. *Large engine air intakes sit above the wing roots;
overhead, almost a delta wing look; refueling probe on starboard
side of nose.*

For years the Navy's standard attack bomber, carrying more than
six tons of armament (including nuclear bombs) on a relatively light
five-ton airframe. The short triangular wings gave it carrier size without the complications of a folding wing, and allowed for integral fuel
tanks throughout the wings. Viewers of news footage from the 1991
Gulf War will see modernized versions of the venerable Skyhawks
(first flown in 1954) in the Kuwaiti air force.

Grumman A-6 Intruder/E-6 Prowler

A-6 specifications: *Length:* 54'7" (16.64 m)   *Wingspan:* 53'
(16.15 m)   *Level flight:* 625 mph (1006 km/h) Mach 0.82 at
sea level

The *twin jet engines mounted at the wing roots,* combined with
swept wings, are diagnostic and give the plane its characteristic,
bulky forward, slim aft look. Up close, note the hooked-nose electronic probe in front of the cockpit.

The Navy's basic night/all-weather bomber since 1960, the A-6A
was heavily used during the Vietnam War along with the newer Air
Force F-111s for night precision bombing. The basic airplane, with
side-by-side seating, has been modified into a radar and communi-
cations jamming craft, the EA-6. A four-seat version, the EA-6B,
has sophisticated antielectronics capacity. Both E versions are distinguished by the electronic pod on the tail fin; what appear to
be externally mounted bombs on the EA-6s are additional wing-
mounted electronics. Electronic jamming Prowlers served in the
1991 Gulf War.

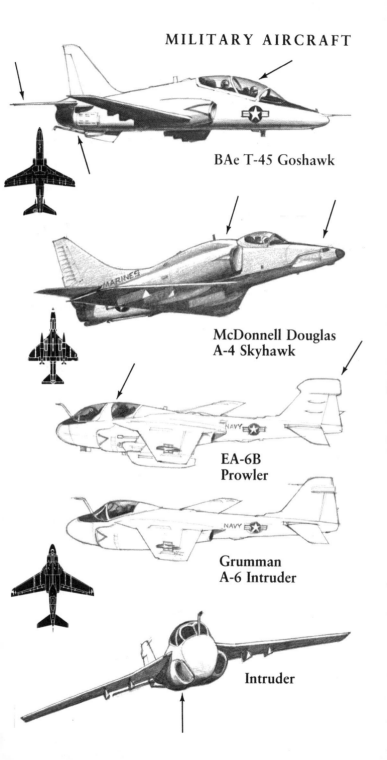

MILITARY AIRCRAFT

BAe T-45 Goshawk

McDonnell Douglas
A-4 Skyhawk

EA-6B
Prowler

Grumman
A-6 Intruder

Intruder

Vought A-7 Corsair II

Length: 46′1″ (14 m)   *Wingspan:* 38′8″ (11.78 m)   *Level flight:* 698 mph (1123 km/h) Mach 0.9 at sea level

Rare. *High-winged; large air intake and exhaust; overhead or on the ground, note the bulky fuselage without any apparent taper.*
Once the Navy's standard attack bomber, based on the older, and supersonic, now retired USAF F-8 design, bulked up for carrier duty. Like its World War II namesake, the old F4-U Corsair, it was a durable weapons platform with a long career. The Corsair II flew from Vietnam through the 1991 Gulf War; the original Corsair was in WWII, Korea, and saw some duty in Vietnam. Now a Naval Reserve and National Guard aircraft.

McDonnell Douglas AV-8B Harrier

Length: 46′4″ (14.1 m)   *Wingspan:* 30′4″ (9.23 m)   *Level flight:* 655 mph (1055 km/h) Mach 0.89 at sea level

Unmistakable, the Harrier has *huge air intakes extending from the wing root halfway to the nose,* giving it a very pointed nose when seen from below; a *bulbous canopy* makes it look a little more conventional from the side. *High, stubby wings carry four hardpoints;* these are noticeable even when the plane is not armed.
First flown at the Paris Air Show in the 1960s, a British Harrier I astonished the crowd by taking off vertically — the first fixed-wing attack aircraft in the world with no-runway, zero-roll capability. Now the workhorse of the U.S. Marines for forward air support, after a long struggle with the Navy, which wanted to keep combat support purely in Navy hands, and with Washington, where bureaucrats didn't want to import the Hawker Siddley (British Aerospace) design. A joint venture with McDonnell Douglas solved the problem.

McDonnell Douglas F-4 Phantom

Length: 58–63′ (17.7–19.2 m)   *Wingspan:* 38′4″ (11.7 m)
Level flight: up to 1500 mph (2414 km/h) Mach 2.25 at altitude

Scarce and disappearing in the United States. Look for the Phantom near Air National Guard and Marine Corps Reserve fields and practice ranges: *Drooping tail planes and upswept wing tips;* overhead, a *deep triangular wing and comparatively small tail plane.*
A very large carrier-based aircraft, also once flown as a part of the USAF. The fighter-bomber versions carried as much as eight tons of munitions, more than the payload of a WWII B-29 Superfortress. It was once the basic interceptor, fighter-bomber, and electronic reconnaissance aircraft for both the Navy and the Air Force, which accounts for the many nose configurations (see sketches). Still flown by several foreign air forces.

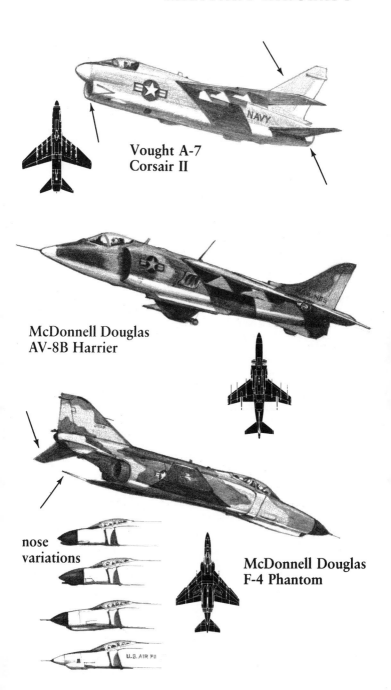

MILITARY AIRCRAFT

Vought A-7
Corsair II

McDonnell Douglas
AV-8B Harrier

nose
variations

McDonnell Douglas
F-4 Phantom

Northrop F-5 Tiger II/Talon T-38 trainer

Length: 46'–51' (14.0 m–15.5 m)   *Wingspan:* 25'–26' (7.6 m–37.9 m)   *Level flight:* E version, 1060 mph (1706 km/h) Mach 1.6 at altitude

The T-38 version was used for ten years by the USAF Thunderbirds precision flying team at airshows; the fighter-interceptor versions are very rare in the U.S. The *small, oval engine intakes* and the simple, almost *triangular, wing and tail planes* are unique among military aircraft.

More than a thousand T-38s were used by the Air Force and Navy as trainers, and several thousand versions of the F-5 have been sold with Defense Department subsidies to noncommunist air forces throughout the world. About 100 F-5Es equipped with radar and weapons systems that mimic Russian equipment are based at Nellis Air Force Base, in Nevada, and at Miramar Naval Air Station, in California, where they are used in war games to imitate Russian MiG-21 fighters. F-5s have been manufactured under license in Canada and are in service with the Canadian Defence Force.

General Dynamics F-16 Fighting Falcon

Length: 46'6" (14.2 m)   *Wingspan:* 31' (9.45 m)   *Level flight:* 1300 mph (2092 km/h) Mach 1.96 at altitude

Widely seen. The USAF Thunderbirds have flown the F-16 since 1983. Head on, note the "shark's mouth" air intake and *the drooping tail plane;* in side view, the plane appears to perch on top of the engine and shows a pair of *keel-like stabilizers* below the tail assembly; overhead, the *clipped triangular wing and tail planes* are diagnostic.

A bundle of graphite-epoxy wrapped around an afterburning turbofan jet engine, the F-16 started out as an experimental design to test lightweight construction techniques and ended up as the Air Force's choice as a combat fighting machine over battlefield areas. Since its adoption in 1975, the Air Force has turned it into a fighter-bomber and long-range interceptor, adding to its weight and cutting its maneuverability.

McDonnell Douglas–Northrop F-18 Hornet

Length: 65' (17.07 m)   *Wingspan:* 37'6" (11.43 m)   *Level flight:* 1190 mph (1915 km/h) Mach 1.8 at altitude

One of the most easily identified of modern jet fighters: *Half-round air intakes; twin tail fins lean outward; needle nose sweeps into a fairing into the wing;* overhead, *stubby, clipped, triangular wings and strongly swept tail planes.*

Because more news clips were broadcast from aircraft carriers than from land bases during the 1991 Gulf War, it sometimes seemed that the F-18 was the only American fighter-bomber in the theater. Originally intended to be a single-seater, but two-seat trainers and fighter-bombers have been produced. Although designed for aircraft carriers, it is the fighter of choice in Canada (replacing F-101s, F-104s and F-5s) and in Australia, where it is produced under license. Flown by the U.S. Navy's Blue Angels demonstration team.

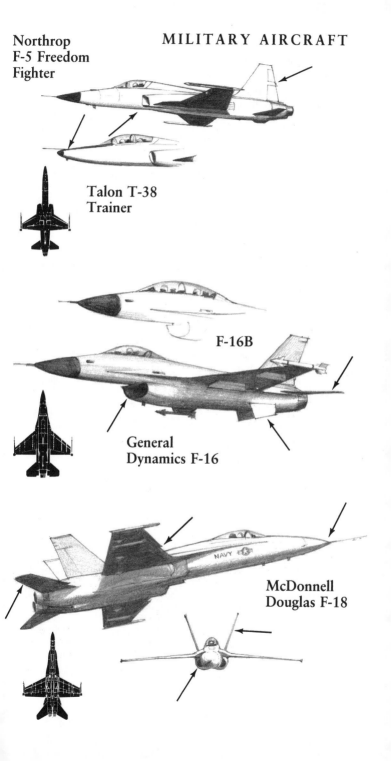

MILITARY AIRCRAFT

Northrop
F-5 Freedom
Fighter

Talon T-38
Trainer

F-16B

General
Dynamics F-16

McDonnell
Douglas F-18

NAVY

McDonnell Douglas F-15 Eagle

Length: 63'8" (19.42 m)   *Wingspan:* 42'8" (13.0 m)   *Level flight:*
1650 mph (2655 km/h) Mach 2.5 at altitude

Increasingly common. *Massive rectangular engine air intakes; wing
and tail planes of multifaceted geometry;* and *twin vertical tail fins.*

This airplane gives the impression of a great deal of mechanism
crammed close together. The small cockpit seems to bubble up higher
and more abruptly than on any other modern jet fighter. A training
version has two seats in tandem. The appearance of a large amount
of engine and a small amount of airframe is indicative of the plane's
performance: It is faster than all but the most advanced Russian
MiG-25s and much more maneuverable than they are at high speeds.
May be seen with a bulge along the outside of each engine housing,
indicating removable fuel tanks. These give the plane a maximum
range of nearly 4000 miles.

Grumman F-14 Tomcat

Length: 61'10" (18.85 m)   *Wingspan:* fully spread, 64'1" (19.5 m);
fully swept, 38'2" (11.63 m)   *Level flight:* 1560 mph (2510 km/h)
Mach 2.35 at altitude

A complex variable-wing plane. On first view, compare the F-15
Eagle and F-18 Hornet before deciding; on the flight line, *twin tail
fins angle out slightly, rectangular air intakes angle inward at the top.*
When the wings are extended at takeoff and landing, note the *bulky
wing roots* housing the variable geometry mechanism.

When the F-111 swept-wing proved much too heavy for carrier
basing, the Navy chose the F-14 from a design competition. Separating Navy F-14s from Air Force F-15s by service markings will become increasingly difficult as planes are stripped of any distinctive
painted markings that would make them identifiable on radar. F-15
Eagles have a smaller bubble canopy for a single pilot, whereas the
F-14 carries a pilot and a radar intercept officer under a longer
canopy.

General Dynamics F-111, FB-111, and EF-111

Length: 73'6" (22.40 m)   *Wingspan:* fully spread, 63' (19.2 m),
fully swept, 31'11" (9.74 m)   *Level flight:* 1650 mph (2655 km/h)
Mach 2.4 at altitude

On the ground or near the base, *thin swept wings* jut out of the
bulky wing roots housing the variable geometry mechanism; in side
view, note a curious asymmetrical sculpting of the nose.

The F-111, developed as a supersonic fighter-bomber, has evolved
into a less common medium-range bomber (FB-111) and, in the EF
configuration, as a radar suppressor and target locater. The rare EFs
are distinguished by an electronic pod in the upper tail fin. What we
have here is essentially a half-sized B-1 bomber (or perhaps the B-1 is
an oversized F-111). Although one is unlikely to see an F-111 in the
fully swept mode (the plane will be very high and going very fast) it
would be separable from delta-wing planes by the notched effect
where the wing meets the tail plane and by the clipped-off tail planes.

MILITARY AIRCRAFT

McDonnell
Douglas F-15 Eagle

Grumman F-14
Tomcat

General
Dynamics F-111

FB-111

EF-111A

Lockheed S-3 Viking

Length: 53′4″ (16.26 m)   *Wingspan:* 68′8″ (20.93 m)   *Level flight:* 506 mph (814 km/h) Mach 0.76 at altitude

Note the *twin jet engines pylon-mounted down and forward of the wing* and the *unswept wings;* overhead, it has noticeably *greater wingspan than length.*

When seen on alert, a long magnetic detecting boom extends to 15 feet behind the tail. A carrier-based antisubmarine-warfare craft with a crew of four, it has the same mission as the land-based, turboprop Orion P-3 Electra. It is remarkably maneuverable for a reconnaissance aircraft, capable of dropping to sea level from 30,000 feet in two minutes. In addition to magnetic detection, the S-3 has side- and forward-looking radar and infrared capacity. Conversions to passenger and cargo uses for delivery to aircraft carriers are coming into service.

Lockheed U-2R, TR-1, ER-1

Length: 49′7″ (15.11 m)   *Wingspan:* 80′ (24.38 m)   *Cruising speed:* 460 mph (740 km/h) Mach 0.69 at altitude

Very unusual configuration. *Single jet engine* and *80-foot wingspan are unique.* The *sensor pods on the wings are integral,* not mounted on pylons. Some appear in civilian dress as environmental research (ER-1) aircraft. Mission pods vary.

The U-2, first flown in 1955, continues to be produced as a platform for aerial observation from the ordinarily safe height of 80,000 feet or more. In addition to the Air Force, NASA and other civilian agencies fly ER-1 for high-altitude scientific research. New versions, equipped with side-looking radar and laser equipment for selecting targets and guiding missiles and bombs to them are designated TR-1. Large, wing-mounted fuel tanks give the U-2 the appearance of a twin jet when seen overhead. As scientific aircraft, they occasionally appear at civilian airports.

Douglas A-3 Skywarrior

Length: 76′4″ (23.27 m)   *Wingspan:* 72′6″ (22.1 m)   *Level flight:* 610 mph (981 km/h) Mach 0.79 at sea level

Scarce. Note the long, thin *swept wings with engines mounted well forward.* The wings enter the fuselage *without fairings.*

The A-3 was designed in 1952 as the first all-jet nuclear bomber to fly from a carrier deck and is the heaviest carrier-borne aircraft in any navy. But, as bombs got lighter and aircraft more sophisticated, it has been relegated entirely to mission support, either as a pure in-air refueling tanker or as a combination tanker–radar suppression plane. A few of the originals are seen near naval air bases, where they are used in multiengine training.

MILITARY AIRCRAFT

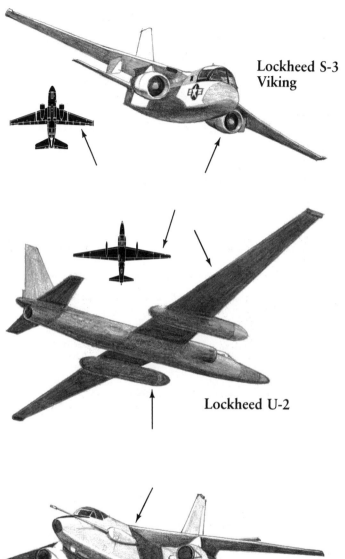

Lockheed S-3
Viking

Lockheed U-2

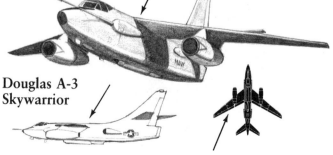

Douglas A-3
Skywarrior

Lockheed C-5A Galaxy

Length: 247'10" (75.54 m)   *Wingspan:* 222'8" (67.87 m)   *Cruising speed:* long range, 518 mph (833 km/h) Mach 0.78 at altitude

Uncommon. Compare the C-141 StarLifter (next entry) before deciding. *Massive fuselage* with *high wing* and *T-tail. Four turbofan engines* (noticeably larger in front, tapering to aft); overhead, compare the Boeing 747 silhouette (page 168).

The largest, and certainly the loudest, aircraft in North America, the C-5A is an awesome sight on takeoff, with flaps fully extended and four engines generating more than twice the noise of a Boeing 747. Viewed overhead, it can be distinguished from the 747 (both have engines that taper noticeably from front to back, unlike the C-141's) by the wing shape: There is very little fairing, or widening, of the wing root on the C-5A as it enters the fuselage.

Lockheed C-141A StarLifter (and stretched C-141B)

Length: C-141A, 145' (44.2 m); C-141B, 168'4" (51.28 m)
Wingspan: both models, 159'10" (48.74 m)   *Cruising speed:* 495 mph (796 km/h) Mach 0.75 at altitude

Based nationwide. On the ground, one of three *high-wing, four-jet, T-tail* planes in North America. See the similar C5-A Galaxy and C-17 (this page) for comparison. Confusing overhead, but the bulges under and just aft of the *moderately swept wings* house the landing gear.

The Air Force's basic cargo and passenger aircraft, the jumbo-jet-sized C-141 differs from all commercial four-engine jets by the combination of the high wing and T-tail. Within a few years, all the C-141s will be stretched into the B versions, which also have a domed fairing to house an in-flight refueling receptacle on the top of the fuselage just aft of the cockpit. Like many commercial jets, the original C-141 had more lifting capacity than cabin capacity; the same solution so common in airliners, stretching, though it improved total load capacity, did not solve the problem created by the narrow cross section of the fuselage, which keeps it from carrying bulky items, such as full-sized tanks.

McDonnell Douglas C-17

Length: 174' (53.04 m)   *Wingspan:* 165' (50.29 m)   *Estimated speeds:* 403 mph (648 km/h) at low altitude, Mach 0.7 at high altitude

New in 1991, thus very rare. *Huge, very fat fuselage; enormous, high tail fin is deeper at the top; upswept fuselage; large fairings under wing for landing gear.*

The C-17 is a cross, in many senses, between the short-field C-130 Hercules, which is too narrow for carrying outsized combat equipment, and the wide-body C-5, which requires a long paved runway. Design requirements are to carry, for example, three Bradley Fighting Vehicles or an M1 battle tank plus support gear, with a maximum short-range payload of 172,000 pounds (78,108 kg), and to land that load on a forward airstrip only 3000 feet (914 m) long.

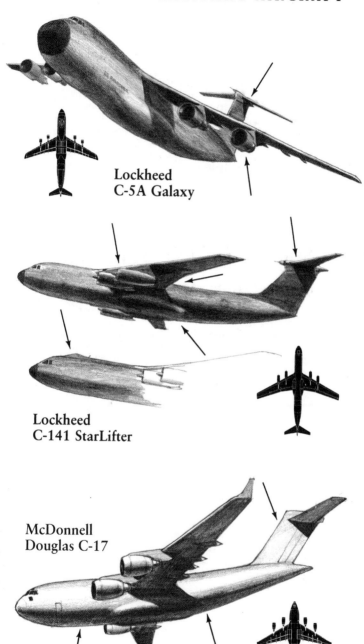

MILITARY AIRCRAFT

Lockheed
C-5A Galaxy

Lockheed
C-141 StarLifter

McDonnell
Douglas C-17

Boeing B-52 Stratofortress

Length: 157'7" (48 m)   *Wingspan:* 185' (56.39 m)   *Level flight:* 650 mph (1046 km/h) Mach 0.98 at altitude

Eight engines are carried in pairs below and forward of the wings' leading edges. Overhead, the contrails frequently show the eight exhausts, but note the *unfaired swept wings, illusion of four engines;* on the flight line, *droopy-winged.*

Of the more than 550 B-52s built in the 1950s and early 1960s, a few hundred remain in service. Current models may show a bulge below the cockpit, housing forward-looking radar or low-light television. Many carry two air-to-surface missiles between the outboard engines and the wing tips. Many will be seen with a dozen wing-mounted, short-range Cruise missiles. Some current models may be carrying a number of wing-mounted rockets intended to divert heat-seeking surface-to-air antiaircraft missiles.

Rockwell B-1

Length: 143' (43.58 m)   *Wingspan:* fully spread, 137' (41.75 m); fully swept, 78' (23.77 m)   *Level flight:* 1454 mph (2339 km/h) Mach 2.19 at altitude; subsonic at sea level

Huge, the size of a Boeing 707 or a stretched DC9 Super 80, with *four engines mounted in pairs near the wing roots; wings extend for landing and takeoff, sweep back for operational flight;* a sculptural quality to the drooping nose and fuselage-to-wing area; two *beard-like winglets under the "chin"* and a *bulletlike "closeout" fairing to the tail end of the fuselage.*

This plane will be produced in small numbers, but will attract attention by its size alone. You are unlikely to see it except with the wings fully extended unless you are near desert testing areas, where it will be executing supersonic, low-level maneuvers. On the ground, its massive, tall landing gear gives it a birdlike pose.

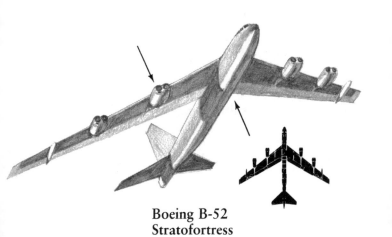

**Boeing B-52
Stratofortress**

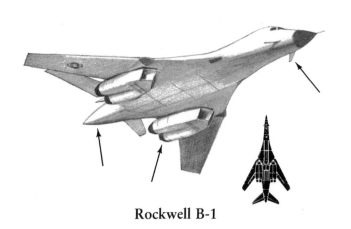

Rockwell B-1

Lockheed F-117A Stealth Fighter

All specifications remain secret at time of publication; however, the plane is at least 55' (16.76 m) long, and wingspan is estimated at 40' (12.2 m). Speed unknown, but probably in the range of 560 mph (902 km/h), Mach 0.85.

A bizarre plane with *no curved surfaces anywhere.*

First of all, it isn't even a fighter. It's a very small, long-range, radar-evading bomber, meant to carry a few "smart" bombs into heavily defended airspace. The plane is covered with a radar-absorbing material that is gooped on after construction and replaced frequently. The material gives the plane an odd optical effect: It will appear as any color, from reddish brown to neutral black. Used successfully for the first time in the 1991 Gulf War.

Northrop B-2 Stealth Bomber

Estimated specifications: *Length:* 69' (21.03 m)   *Wingspan:* 172' (52.43 m)   *Speed:* 570 mph (1010 km/h)

The only *flying wing* the width of a football field.

Residents of southern California desert communities have now seen three flying wings since the 1940s, all Northrops: The pusher-propeller B-35 and the jet B-49 were canceled years ago, and the B-2 may never get past the production of a few prototypes, given the breakup of the Soviet Union and the absence of a sophisticated enemy. The double air intakes and exhausts each house a pair of jet engines, so the B-2 is actually a four-engine aircraft. Yes, it can fly.

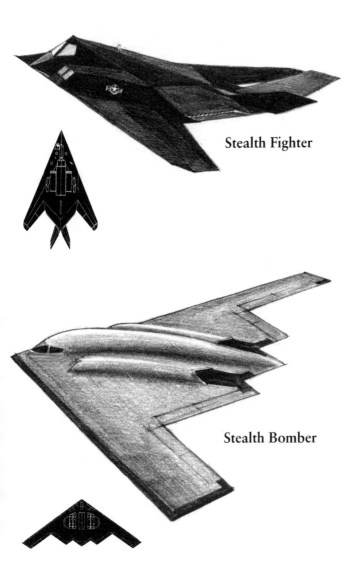

Stealth Fighter

Stealth Bomber

Bell Model 47

Length: 43'7" (13.30 m)   *Main rotor diameter:* 37'1" (11.32 m)
Cruising speed: 84 mph (135 km/h)   *Useful load:* 1025 lbs
(416 kg)   pilot, two passengers

For decades, this craft defined "helicopter." The *huge one-piece bubble extends to the cabin deck,* giving the craft a much more *round-nosed look* than the Lama/Alouettes it resembles.

When in military service, it was called the AH-1 Sioux, and in its medical evacuation role it starred in the opening sequence of the television series *M*A*S*H.* Various models were produced from 1945 to 1974, and many were converted for special uses, including the Continental "El Tomcat" agricultural sprayer with a roll-bar cage cabin and a pointed nose replacing the Plexiglas bubble.

Aerospatiale SA-315B Lama

Length: 42'4" (12.91 m)   *Main rotor diameter:* 36'1" (11.02 m)
Cruising speed: 75 mph (120 km/h)   *Useful load:* 2050 lbs (929 kg)
crew of two, three passengers

One of two modern copters with the *lattice work of the tail boom exposed to view.* The Lama (and earlier Alouettes) have a *multipane bubbled canopy that stops well above the bottom of the cabin.*

The most recent of a line of French-designed, Texas-built helicopters (it's basically an Alouette II frame with an Alouette III power plant), the Lama has a certified ceiling of 17,715 feet (5400 m) but has landed and taken off in the Himalayas at 24,600 feet (7500 m). It's a popular Alpine rescue helicopter, and is named (in English spelling) for the Andean two-*l* llama, not the one-*l* Tibetan religious leader.

Hiller UH-12

Length: 40'8" (12.41 m)   *Main rotor diameter:* 35'5" (10.80 m)
Cruising speed: 90 mph (154 km/h)   *Useful load:* 1341 lbs (608 kg)
crew of two, three passengers

Of all the slim-tailed small helicopters, only the UH-12 has a *bent-up tail boom braced with a spar running from just below the main rotor to the top of the tail.*

The original UH-12 (designated Hiller 360) was the military's H-23 "Raven." Out of production for a decade, it has been revived, and many UH-12s now have turboshaft engines. The UH-12 is used primarily as an agricultural sprayer and seeder.

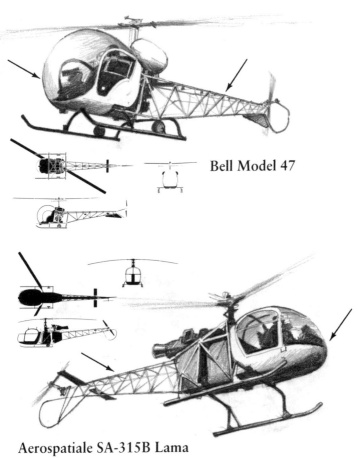

Bell Model 47

Aerospatiale SA-315B Lama

Hiller UH-12

Schweizer Model 300 (Hughes 269/300)

Length: 30'10" (9.4 m)   *Main rotor diameter:* 26'10" (8.18 m)
Cruising speed: 77 mph (124 km/h)   pilot, two passengers

Oval *windows* in the doors give this aircraft the most *dragonfly-looking* head of all helicopters, especially when combined with the *slim tail boom braced from beneath the fuselage.*

Developed in the 1950s, the Hughes 269/300 was employed as the TH 55A "Osage," the U.S. Army's basic helicopter trainer. The Schweizer Corporation has concentrated, with much success, on supplying police versions with some armor plating and special floodlighting and public-address systems. The slightly larger Schweizer 330 shows a small window behind the door, making it look like what it is, something halfway between a Schweizer 300 and the Hughes/McDonnell Douglas 500.

Robinson 22

Length: 28'9" (8.76 m)   *Main rotor diameter:* 25'2" (7.67 m)
Cruising speed: 108 mph (174 km/h)   *Useful load:* 538 lbs (244 kg)
two pilots (dual controls standard)

It's the most recently designed small helicopter, and looks the most modern: *slim unbraced tail cone, tall streamlined main rotor pylon, simple two-piece canopy bubble.* The exposed *engine showing below the tail boom* breaks the smooth surface, but the design cuts down cabin noise and makes maintenance easier.

Designed from scratch for the civilian market in the 1970s, the Robinson 22 emphasized low maintenance, relatively quiet operation, and high speed. It is a popular trainer and police vehicle. Near fishing ports, many float-equipped models are used for tuna and swordfish spotting. Holds numerous performance records for its class of small helicopters.

McDonnell Douglas MD 500, 530 (Hughes 500)

MD 500 specifications: *Length:* 30'10" (9.40 m)   *Main rotor diameter:* 26'4" (8.03 m)   *Cruising speed:* 137 mph (220 km/h)
Useful load: 1559 lbs (707 kg)   various passenger loads; maximum, pilot, six passengers

Distinctive *sharp-nosed multipane canopy, glass to deck; irregular large windows in each of four doors.* Earlier Hughes models had a rounded nose, but similar door-window treatment. Later 500 and 530 models have a *T-tail horizontal stabilizer above the tail rotor.* The long slim boom is fully faired into the fuselage.

Widely seen as a commuter carrier and executive aircraft in the United States. Versions of the basic MD 500 are in military service in several foreign countries, marketed with TOW missile mounts as the "Defender." The earlier Hughes 500 was the U.S. Army's OH-6 "Cayuse."

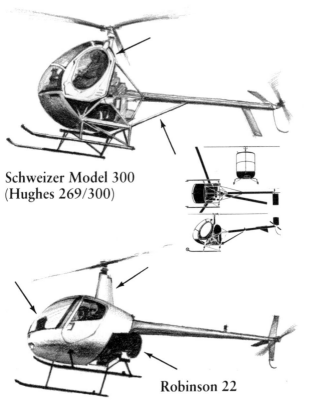

**Schweizer Model 300
(Hughes 269/300)**

Robinson 22

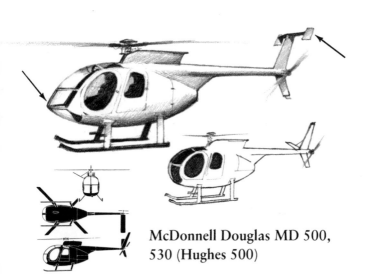

**McDonnell Douglas MD 500,
530 (Hughes 500)**

Enstrom 280FX, F28F

280FX specifications: *Length:* 29'4" (8.7 m)   *Main rotor diameter:* 32'0" (9.75 m)   *Cruising speed:* 107 mph (172 km/h)   *Useful load:* 1015 lbs (460 kg)   pilot, one passenger

Graceful nose; two small teardrop look-down windows at the pilot's feet are distinctively Enstrom (the Fairchild 1100, by comparison, has large rhomboid look-downs). Model F-28s have a huge side window filling the door frame; on 280s, the window stops at the cabin midline. The 280's nose extends gracefully; the F28 is snubbier.

Enstrom, a small company founded by the aviator and inventor Rudolf Enstrom, had produced about 1000 helicopters by 1991, and has been owned at different times by two corporations and a group of private investors, including F. Lee Bailey, the celebrity lawyer. Recent models have improved passenger comfort and reduced noise emissions, but the aircraft look similar to older models.

Brantly-Hynes B-2

Length: 28'0" (8.53 m)   *Main rotor diameter:* 23'99" (7.24 m) *Cruising speed:* 90 mph (145 km/h)   *Useful load:* 610 lbs (276 kg) dual-control two-seater

The B-2 and the Brantly-Hynes 305 (next entry) have tail cones that seem to grow out of the fuselage, and combined with the *double-bulge Plexiglas canopy,* they look like aluminum ice cream cones with a scoop of glass on top. The *half-round door windows* are unique to Brantly-Hynes copters.

Produced by an Oklahoma company that turned out a few dozen helicopters annually for 20 years, and now manufactured under license in India. All of the B-2s were delivered with small tail wheels on their skids.

Brantly-Hynes 305

Length: 32'11" (10.03 m)   *Main rotor diameter:* 28'8" (8.74 m) *Cruising speed:* 110 mph (177 km/h)   *Useful load:* 900 lbs (408 kg)   crew of two, three passengers

This is the jumbo ice cream cone, with *odd-geometry passenger windows* showing behind *half-round door windows.* Standard model delivered with *unusual fixed tricycle gear,* but even on floats, it would look like a Brantly-Hynes.

A few dozen B-H 305s survive in the United States and Canada, most in corporate "executive" service. International travelers may remember them as airline connectors at Heathrow, England.

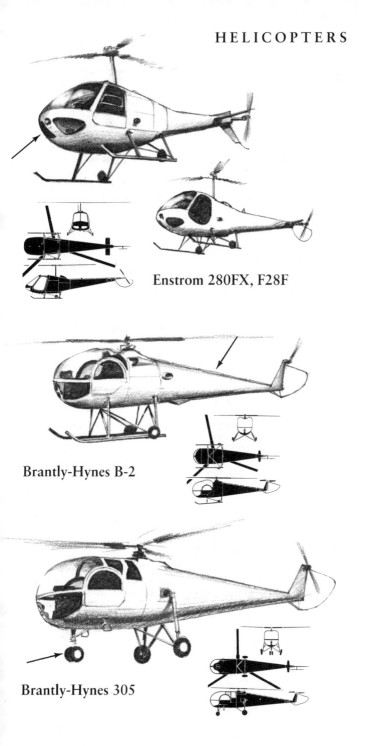

Enstrom 280FX, F28F

Brantly-Hynes B-2

Brantly-Hynes 305

Hiller FH-1100 Pegasus

Length: 41'3" (12.57 m)   *Main rotor diameter:* 35'5" (10.80 m)
Cruising speed: 122 mph (196 km/h)   *Useful load:* 1030 lbs
(468 kg)   pilot, four passengers

Not common. *Low, almost horizontal tail boom emerges from the bottom of the bulky fuselage.* A large *L-shaped exhaust* shows below the main rotor, and the *engine location is clearly visible, above the fuselage.*

This infrequently encountered craft was developed for a military competition — a fly-off for an observation and light-transport vehicle. The winner was the Vietnam-era Hughes OH-6 Cayuse (unofficially named the "Loach" in country; see earlier entry for McDonnell Douglas/Hughes 500). Although much modified since the original military model, the unique overall shape of the Pegasus is unchanged.

MBB BO 105

Length: 38'11" (11.86 m)   *Main rotor diameter:* 32'3" (9.83 m)
Cruising speed: 127 mph (204 km/h)   *Useful load:* 2425 lbs
(1100 kg)   pilot, four passengers

Combines a *deep fuselage* with a *short-looking horizontal tail boom set high under the main rotor; large airscoop in front of the rotor drive shaft.* Rear passenger-door window is much smaller than the one in the pilot's door. The largest model (LSB, illustrated) has a cabin that is a foot longer than standard, and has a *third small side window.* Small *"end-plate fins" on horizontal stabilizer.* When the aircraft is stopped, note the *non-drooping, rigid rotors.*

This German invention (MBB stands for Messerschmitt-Bolkow-Blohm) is manufactured in Canada as well as in Germany. The rigid main rotors can be pitched to push the craft down (other helicopters can rise or sink, but not achieve negative g), making it capable of ground-hugging flight in combat, less sensitive to downdrafts, and quicker when moving from assigned altitude to ground level. Many in air ambulance and search-and-rescue use.

MBB/Kawasaki BK 117

Length: 42'8" (13 m)   *Main rotor diameter:* 36'1" (11 m)   *Cruising speed:* 158 mph (264 km/h)   *Useful load:* 1948 lbs (917 kg)   pilot, seven passengers

Not common, but noticeable and distinctive. *Large pod fuselage, high horizontal tail boom, huge angled vertical stabilizers.* Also note the large air intake and visible exhaust pipe just below the *always horizontal rigid rotors.*

This is a joint German-Japanese venture, MBB providing the running gear, Kawasaki the airframe and electronics. Similar to the MBB 105, but with larger engines, more capacity, higher speed. The anticipated military market had not been achieved by 1991. A few of the first 100 produced are in air ambulance service in the United States, and attract attention by their unusual speed.

Hiller FH-1100 Pegasus

MBB BO 105

MBB/Kawasaki BK 117

Aerospatiale Alouette III

Length: 42'1" (12.84 m)   *Main rotor diameter:* 36'1" (11.02 m)
Cruising speed: 122 mph (197 km/h)   *Useful load:* 2386 lbs
(1078 kg)   pilot, up to seven passengers

Uncommon. Note the *very large multipane "greenhouse" canopy.*
Exposed turboshaft engine. Upside-down tail rotor guard also serves
as a landing skid. Standard with *non-retractable tricycle landing gear.*

Astonishing high-altitude performance makes this a popular police
and rescue craft in the European Alps and a small workhorse load-
lifter in the American Rockies. With a crew of two and a 550 pound
(250 kg) payload, this copter took off and landed at 19,698 feet
(6004 m) in the Himalayas.

Aerospatiale Ecureuil 350 (formerly Astar in North America)

Length: 42'7" (12.99 m)   *Main rotor diameter:* 35' (10.68 m)
Cruising speed: 144 mph (232 km/h)   *Useful load:* 1847 lbs
(838 kg)   pilot, five or six passengers

One of the commonest large utility civilian helicopters, with more
than 350 in the United States. *Pointy-nosed; teardrop look-down
windows like nostril openings; enclosed engine;* up close, the *tail rotor drive shaft housing lies on top of the tail cone.* The "Twinstar" is
similar, shows two air intakes and exhausts for its paired engines.

Current production is now "Ecureuil" and "Twinstar" worldwide,
as the Lycoming-powered "Astar" has been superseded by craft with
French-built Turbomeca engines. Aerospatiale builds flyable helicopters in France, where they are test flown in a "green" state, then dis-
assembled, shipped, and reassembled in Texas, where final wiring,
piping, and all avionics are installed, along with customizing details.

Aerospatiale Gazelle

Length: 39'3" (11.97 m)   *Main rotor diameter:* 34'5" (10.50 m)
Cruising speed: 144 mph (233 km/h)   *Useful load:* 1460 lbs
(661 kg)   pilot, four passengers

One of two helicopters with the *tail rotor enclosed in the tail fin*
(see Aerospatiale Dauphin, next entry), the Gazelle has a *huge
bubble-fronted greenhouse canopy;* enclosed *turboshaft engine
stands out behind main rotor drive shaft.* Near at hand, *tail rotor
drive shaft lies on tail cone.* Has a *rigid, non-drooping main rotor*
similar to the MBB series (page 200)

Quite rare in the United States, many more in French and British
military service. The unusual rotor-in-tail, called a "fenestron," was
repeated in the commonly seen, much larger U.S. Coast Guard
Dolphin. No longer produced in North America.

Aerospatiale Alouette III

Aerospatiale Ecureuil 350

Aerospatiale Gazelle

Aerospatiale Dauphin II, USCG HH-65 Dolphin

Length: 45'6" (13.88 m)   *Main rotor diameter:* 39'2" (11.94 m)
Cruising speed: 160 mph (257 km/h)   *Useful load:* 4341 lbs
(1969 kg)   crew of two, 11 passengers

In its Coast Guard red and white, one of the commonest coastal helicopters. The *tall, large tail fin encloses "fenestron" tail rotor, fully retractable gear, end-plated horizontal stabilizer forward of tail fan-rotor.* Civilian versions show various window designs, but the tail end is diagnostic.

Like other Aerospatiale craft, about 40 percent of the value is added in the Texas assembly plant, but it still took a wonderful design to make this the first foreign helicopter to win a U.S. government competition. In addition to Coast Guard short-range ship-based rescue, Dauphin/Dolphins are carried on icebreakers and cutters. Executive versions take advantage of the large cabin to build a sound cocoon that depresses ambient noise to a level equivalent to highway noise inside a luxury sedan.

Agusta A109 Hirundo

Length: 42'9" (13.05 m)   *Main rotor diameter:* 36'1" (11.00 m)
Cruising speed: 144 mph (233 km/h)   *Useful load:* 2600 lbs
(1180 kg)   pilot, seven passengers

One of the few helicopters that is truly *streamlined. Fully retractable landing gear; slim nose; swept-back tail fins; engine, smoothly wrapped, sits just under main rotor.* Compare with Sikorsky Spirit (next entry).

One of Italy's most successful aircraft, the Hirundo carries the president of Italy and dozens of American corporate executives. "Hirundo" is "swallow" in Italian, and this helicopter moves with comparable rapidity. Originally single-engined, everything you see will be twin-engined, for emergency reliability.

Sikorsky S-76 Spirit

Length: 52'6" (16 m)   *Main rotor diameter:* 44' (13.41 m)
Cruising speed: 144 mph (232 km/h)   *Useful load:* 4700 lbs
(2132 kg)   crew of two, up to 12 passengers

Huge, but still streamlined. The Spirit's *tall slim tail fin is all above tail cone; twin engine air intakes obvious below main rotor; odd-geometry side windows;* very unusual *paired look-down windows;* fully *retractable landing gear.*

Sikorsky designed this craft specifically for the support of offshore oil platforms; it is capable of ferrying rig workers and equipment for considerable distances. Many have been modified for air ambulance work, with redundant backup electrical service, suction, and medical gases delivery. Extreme utilization of lightweight materials is typical, and many modifications for increased quiet and dampened vibration have been incorporated since 1980.

Aerospatiale Dauphin II,
USCG HH-65 Dolphin

Agusta A109 Hirundo

Sikorsky S-76 Spirit

Bell 206 JetRanger, LongRanger, OH-58 Kiowa

JetRanger specifications: *Length:* 38'9" (11.82 m)   *Main rotor diameter:* 33'4" (10.16 m)   *Cruising speed:* 133 mph (214 km/h)   *Useful load:* 1745 lbs (791 kg)   pilot, four passengers

Very Bell-looking, with its *dorsal and ventral tail fin, tail plane midway down high-set tail boom.* The seven-passenger LongRanger adds a third side window, end plates on the tail plane/horizontal stabilizers (sketch below 206).

Designed as a military aircraft, but thousands of the civilian versions are in service as ambulances and in police, traffic reporting, and news-gathering roles. Ordered by the military in 1968 after considerable delays and price-overruns by the original competition winner, the Hughes OH-6. The LongRanger is the current production model.

Bell 222

Length: 50'4" (15.36 m)   *Main rotor diameter:* 42' (12.80 m)
Cruising speed: 161 mph (269 km/h)   *Useful load:* 3350 lbs
(1520 kg)   pilot, seven passengers

An aircraft with a number of bumps and projections: *Long pointy nose; retractable landing gear in pods (sponsons) that jut straight out; engine exhausts project out to the side; tail plane sticks out halfway down the tail cone; dorsal and ventral tail fin; odd-geometry side windows.*

The first twin-engined civilian helicopter built in the United States. Numerous in New York, where they are in executive transport and police use. May be fitted with floats or tail-wheeled skids instead of retractable gear. The landing gear sponsons are shaped as airfoils, and provide some additional lift in flight.

Aerospatiale 322 Super Puma

Length: 61'4" (18.70 m)   *Main rotor diameter:* 51'2" (15.6 m)
Cruising speed: 165 mph (266 km/h)   *Useful load:* 9128 lbs
(4140 kg)   crew of two, up to 21 passengers

Uncommon in North America. Note the *twin engines mounted well forward, almost in line with main rotor shaft; vented, slatted horizontal stabilizer on port side; large ventral fin/tail skid.* Also, retractable tricycle landing gear and an additional, *much larger side window than on AS 330 Puma.*

More common in Western Europe, where it is in military, VIP, and commuter airline use. The Super Puma was the first and, as of this edition, the only helicopter certified to fly into known or predicted icing conditions. For that reason, it is a common sight at ports surrounding the North Sea petroleum fields, serving as a platform-crew airbus.

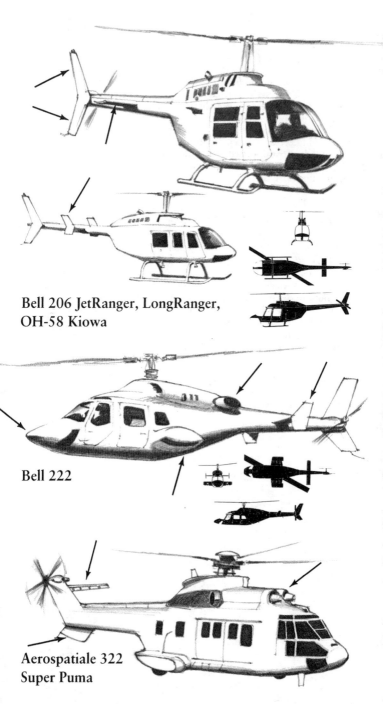

Bell 206 JetRanger, LongRanger, OH-58 Kiowa

Bell 222

Aerospatiale 322 Super Puma

Bell 212, 412

412 specifications: *Length:* 56' (17.07 m)   *Main rotor diameter:* 46'
(14.02 m)   *Cruising speed:* 161 mph (269 km/h)   *Useful load:*
4233 lbs (1920 kg)   crew of two, up to 12 passengers

Most modern of the Bell 204/UH-1 Huey series; see additional
side-view silhouettes for details. The 412 shows a *four-bladed main
rotor and well-streamlined engine housings.*

The 212/412 series started with the old model 204 Uh-1 Huey,
which grew into the longer, slimmer model 205 UH-1 Iroquois. The
big change to 212 added twin engines for redundant reliability and
increased performance. The 412's four-bladed rotor increased performance and decreased fuselage vibration. Versions are manufactured in
several countries. Armed Hueys and Iroquois are rare now; many
have been upgraded and converted for military medical evacuation
and light transport.

Bell 214 ST

Length: 62'2" (18.95 m)   *Main rotor diameter:* 52' (15.85 m)
Cruising speed: 161 mph (295 km/h)   *Useful load:* 4233 lbs
(1920 kg)   crew of two, 18 passengers

*Huge and pointy-nosed; four side windows; tail rotor mounted on
top of tail; long engine fairing with large airscoops and exhausts.*
The 214 was designed for the Shah of Iran as a troop transport to
be built under license in Iran. The fundamentalist revolution inter-
vened, and the 214's actual first use was as a petroleum platform service bus in the North Sea. May be delivered with wheels instead of
skids (for airport transportation), and has been provided with optional de-icing apparatus for Arctic work, including the Alaskan
North Slope oil field.

HELICOPTERS

Bell 212, 412

Bell 204, UH-1 Huey

Bell 205, UH-1 Iroquois

Bell 214 ST

Bell OH-58D Kiowa, SeaRanger

Length: 40'11" (12.49 m)   *Main rotor diameter:* 35'4" (10.77 m)
Cruising speed: 117 mph (188 km/h)   *Useful load:* 1736 lbs
(696 kg)   crew of two

It looks like a Bell 206 JetRanger that had a bad experience in a
body shop: *Flat platform tops a massive engine housing; mast-
mounted "eyeball" gun sight typical; armament sponsons project below cockpit.*

Technically, it's a scout helicopter, but can be armed with air-to-air
or air-to-ground missiles, multiple machine guns, all sighted through
the mast-mounted television eye, built for normal optical or infrared
imaging. Used in the Gulf War, prior to the invasion of Kuwait, to
suppress gunboat attacks on oil tankers. Rarer than the Apache or
HueyCobra attack helicopters.

Bell AH-1 HueyCobra, Seacobra, Super Cobra

HueyCobra specifications: *Length:* 53'1" (16.18 m)   *Main rotor
diameter:* 44' (13.41 m)   *Cruising speed:* 141 mph (227 km/h)
Useful load: 3377 lbs (1531 kg)   crew of two in tandem seats

Earlier single-engined models show *single large exhaust tilted up
behind engine; all have flat-glass cockpit panes.* All have a distinct
pointed nose with prominent chin-turret. Twin-engined Super Cobras
are the Marines' vehicle of choice, and have *large twin engine pods,
cheek bulges* for avionics, *rounded glass cockpit.*

An attack helicopter developed in the 1970s, with many upgrades
including dual engines, more armor, marine avionics, large TOW
missile pods. Also prominent in Desert Storm operations.

McDonnell Douglas AH-64 Apache

Length: 58'3" (17.76 m)   *Main rotor diameter:* 48' (14.63 m)
Cruising speed: 184 mph (296 km/h)   *Useful load:* 3685 lbs
(1671 kg)   pilot and copilot/gunner in tandem seating (pilot in rear)

There are two Army attack helicopters seen near bases in the
United States. This one has wheels (reversed fixed tricycle gear); the
Bell AH-1 HueyCobra doesn't. And this is the one that can fly upside
down, a stunt sometimes performed at air shows. Otherwise, *huge
armored engine nacelles over stubby outrigger wings; angular greenhouse cockpit; bumps and lumps* for avionics and weapon systems;
and rarest of all helicopter gear, a *tail wheel.*

In service since the mid-1980s, and a very successful machine in
Operation Desert Storm, the Apache looks like hell on wheels when
stripped; when armed with rocket launchers, like hell itself. Like the
MBBs, it can fly in negative g — that is, it can push itself down.

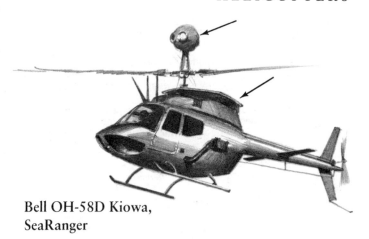

Bell OH-58D Kiowa,
SeaRanger

Bell AH-1 HueyCobra,
SeaCobra, Super Cobra

McDonnell Douglas AH-64 Apache

Kaman H-2 Seasprite

Length: 52'7" (16.03 m)   *Main rotor diameter:* 44' (13.41 m)
Cruising speed: 150 mph (241 km/h)   *Useful load:* 6260 lbs
(2940 kg)   pilot, copilot, sensor operator

Never seen except in Navy paint! *Curious cut-back vertical stabilizer, very small horizontal stabilizers, twin engines with side-venting exhaust, retractable gear; many pods, weapons points, and sensors visible.*
First upgrade was to twin engines, with subsequent increases in speed, range, armament, carrying power. Various models perform over-horizon fleet protection, submarine hunting, search and rescue.

Sikorsky S-62, HH-52A

Length: 45'5" (13.86 m)   *Main rotor diameter:* 53' (16.16 m)
Cruising speed: 98 mph (158 km/h)   *Useful load:* 3017 lbs
(1368 kg)   crew of two, 10 passengers

Rare, declining numbers in Coast Guard red and white; scattered offshore oil use. *Single air intake directly over cockpit; floats on outrigger braces; four symmetrical side windows; single horizontal stabilizer on port side; boat-type hull.*
First delivered to the U.S. Coast Guard in 1963, it is being phased out in favor of more reliable twin-engine craft in both government and private service. Its amphibious ability (no extra flotation devices required) made it the choice, in the sixties, for transporting passengers between San Francisco and Oakland airports.

Sikorsky S-61, SH-3 SeaKing

SeaKing specifications: *Length:* 72'8" (22.15 m)   *Main rotor diameter:* 62' (18.90 m)   *Cruising speed:* 136 mph (219 km/h)
Useful load: 8635 lbs (3618 kg)   military crews vary; civilian versions carried up to 30 passengers

Both commercial and military versions have a *boat-shaped hull,* but civilian versions were not all waterproofed. SeaKings have *flotation pods on outriggers.* Civilian versions showed up to nine side windows.
These were the giant helicopters, in civilian dress, that used to rattle Manhattan's windows between the Pan Am building and La Guardia Airport. They were the first Navy helicopters capable of searching for, and carrying the weapons to destroy, submarines.

Sikorsky S-61R HH-3 Pelican, Jolly Green Giant

Length: 73' (22.25 m)   *Main rotor diameter:* 62' (18.90 m)
Cruising speed: 144 mph (232 km/h)   *Useful load:* 8795 lbs
(3990 kg)   normally, crew of two plus engineer/flight chief, up to 30 troops may be carried

If the big red stripe doesn't convince you this is the Coast Guard's Pelican, note the *slim tail boom, larger flotation pontoons, and the sharp cutaway for hydraulic doors at the rear of the fuselage.* In camouflage color, it's an Air National Guard or Air Force Reserve Jolly Green Giant.

Kaman SH-2 Seasprite

Sikorsky S-62, HH-52A

**Sikorsky S-61,
SH-3 SeaKing**

Sikorsky S-61R HH-3 Pelican, Jolly Green Giant

Sikorsky S-70, UH60 Blackhawk, CH-60 Seahawk, Jayhawk

UH60-A specifications: *Length:* 64'10" (19.76 m)   *Main rotor diameter:* 53'8" (16.36 m)   *Cruising speed:* 167 mph (268 km/h)   *Useful load:* 10,716 lbs (4861 kg)   crew of two, plus gunner and up to 14 troops

Note *fixed reversed tricycle landing gear; tail wheel midway down tail cone* (closer to fuselage on Seahawks); *airplane-looking tail unit, tail rotor canted to starboard.* The *side window pattern is distinctive: two small rectangles forward, two large squares in sliding "barn door" entryway.*

Thousands of Blackhawks at U.S. and overseas airborne infantry bases, hundreds more Seahawks at naval bases and aboard frigates, cruisers, and destroyers where they provide air defense radar, anti-submarine capability, and rescue service. Designed in the late seventies for carrying troops into combat, the Blackhawk and its derivatives now mount weapons, deliver mines, and provide both target aquisition and radar suppression for fixed-wing fighter-bombers. First used as the President's personal helicopter in 1989.

Sikorsky S-65, CH-53 Sea Stallion, Super Jolly Green Giant

Stallion specifications: *Length:* 88'3" (26.90 m)   *Main rotor diameter:* 72'3" (22.02 m)   *Cruising speed:* 173 mph (278 km/h)   *Useful load:* 19,556 lbs (8870 kg)   crew of three, 37 troops

Twin engines mounted away from fuselage; blunt nose; high cabin windows; large sponsons; odd one-sided horizontal stabilizer projects to starboard. Later models have canted vertical stabilizer, as does Super Stallion (next entry).

Many fewer CH-53s fly than the Hawk series. Most common near Marine Corps bases. Although built as a large and durable troop carrier, the CH-53 has a very high ceiling and is quite maneuverable. Several have been purchased by Alpine countries as mountain rescue craft. In Navy paint, serves as a transport, rescue platform, and minesweeper.

Sikorsky S-80, CH-53E Super Stallion, Sea Dragon

Length: 99' (30.18 m)   *Main rotor diameter:* 76' (24.08 m)   *Cruising speed:* 173 mph (278 km/h)   *Useful load:* 30,000 (13,607 kg)   crew of three, up to 55 troops

Huge. It's the largest helicopter outside Russia. Sponsons on Marine Corps Super Stallion are larger than on Sea Stallion; Navy's mine-sweeping Sea Dragon (illustrated) has *enormous fuel-holding sponsons.* Projecting to starboard, the *horizontal stabilizer is a "gull wing." Three engines* (third one is on port side, above and behind the others; at rest, *seven-bladed main rotor; vertical tail fin canted to port.*

So totally unlike the CH-53 series Sea Stallions, the Super deserved a military model number of its own, not just the suffix E. Has double the lift capacity, whether you're counting troops or tons, and four times the range of the earlier CH-53s. The Sea Dragon is also used by the Japanese military for submarine hunting and as a minesweeper. The canted tail fin (now being retrofitted on non-Super models) acts as an airfoil, increasing range and lift at altitude.

214

HELICOPTERS

Sikorsky S-70,
H60 Blackhawk,
Seahawk, Jayhawk

Sikorsky S-65, H-53 Sea Stallion,
Super Jolly Green Giant

Sikorsky S-80, H-53E
Super Stallion, Sea Dragon

Sikorsky S-55, H-19 Chickasaw

Length: 57' (17.39 m)   *Main rotor diameter:* 48' (14.63 m)
Cruising speed: 90 mph (145 km/h)   *Useful load:* 1795 lbs
(770 kg)   pilot, up to 10 passengers

A very rare antique. *High cockpit; look-down windows well back on side of cockpit; four-wheel fixed landing gear standard; row of cool-air intakes below cockpit windows; deep fuselage with peculiar bracing fillet marrying fuselage to tail boom.*
This was the first commercial helicopter licensed in the United States. A few hundred civil and a few thousand military versions were built before 1955. It survived for years in the military of small South American countries, and may still be seen in utility roles in rural America.

Sikorsky S-58T, CH-34 Choctaw

Length: 65'10" (20.06 m)   *Main rotor diameter:* 56' (17.07 m)
Cruising speed: 127 mph (204 km/h)   *Useful load:* 5725 lbs
(2596 kg)   pilot, 16 passengers

Quite rare, and non-turbo models (sketch below S-58T) are probably parked for the duration. *High cockpit; long, low, straight fuselage merging into tail cone.* Side windows vary, *six most common; twin "nostril" airscoop for turboshaft engine.*
Successor to the S-55, built in the United States during the 1950s with piston engines. The British-built Westland S-58s had turboshaft engines from the beginning, an idea taken up a decade later here. Although all S-58 production stopped in the early 1960s, Sikorsky continued turbo conversion sales into the late 1970s. About 100 still flying, most now in utility, rather than passenger, roles. Common troop carrier early in Vietnam War.

Sikorsky S-64 Skycrane, CH-54 Tarhe

Length: 88'6" (26.97 m)   *Main rotor diameter:* 72' (21.95 m)
Cruising speed: 109 mph (175 km/h)   *Useful load:* 22,400 lbs
(10,160 kg)   crew of three, with triple controls

Nothing else looks like it. Sharply *cut-out fuselage* is for carrying encapsuled cargo; *long rear "legs" to landing gear.*
A packaged load-lifter, the Skycrane program included a "universal military pod" for cargo or troops and a removable winch system capable of lifting 15,000 pounds (6,800 kg). A few used in civil works, including lifting powerline pylons and delivering bulldozers to isolated sites. Among other signs of lifting power, an unloaded CH-54 has reached an altitude of 11,000 feet (3353 m). Used extensively in Vietnam to move heavy equipment, armored vehicles, and to retrieve crashed airplanes. While the gear is fixed, it is partially retractable, allowing the pilot to settle over, and pick up, the cargo pod.

HELICOPTERS

Sikorsky S-55, H-19 Chickasaw

Sikorsky S-58T,
H-34 Choctaw

Sikorsky S-64 Skycrane,
CH-54 Tarhe

Boeing Vertol/Kawasaki 107, CH-46 Sea Knight

Length: 44'10" (13.66 m)   *Main rotor diameter (each):* 51' (15.5 m)
Cruising speed: 155 mph (249 km/h)   *Useful load:* 9933 lbs
(4506 kg)   crew of two, 25 troops

One of two double-ended helicopters still flying. Sea Knight is *smaller than Chinook* (next entry) and has *large sponsons just forward of the tail, tricycle landing gear,* and side windows are *four round portholes* in rectangular frames.

The Sea Knight was the first replacement for the "Flying Banana" of the Korean War era, but the Army wanted a larger version and opted for the Chinook. The Sea Knight was and remains, after considerable upgrading and refitting, the U.S. Marines' standard medium-size assault helicopter. A few in Navy paint as cargo carriers; even fewer in civilian dress in the United States. Under license, Kawasaki manufactures a military version for Japan, and the only civilian models.

Boeing Model 234, CH-47 Chinook

Latest model CH-47D specifications: *Length:* 99' (30.18 m)   *Main rotor diameter (each):* 60' (18.29 m)   *Cruising speed:* 154 mph (248 km/h)   *Useful load:* 14,160 lbs (6423 kg)   crew of three, up to 55 troops

Compared to the Sea Knight (above): *Continuous bulge along lower sides of fuselage; engines exposed below rear rotor; five round portholes, fixed four-wheel landing gear.* Much rarer civilian versions show more than a dozen rectangular passenger windows on each side.

The workhorse Army troop carrier of the Vietnam War, the Chinook was also used as a heavy cargo transport. More than 400 older Chinooks are being converted to the 47D standard, which almost doubles the useful load and range of the Vietnam-era copters. Civilian versions are in service in the Far East, at both Gulf of Mexico and North Sea ports as airbuses for platform workers, and in the Pacific Northwest as airborne "fire engines."

Kaman H-43 Huskie

Length: 25'2" (7.67 m)   *Main rotor diameter (each):* 47' (14.33 m)
Cruising speed: 98 mph (158 km/h)   *Useful load:* 3800 lbs (1360 kg)
crew of two, up to ten troops

Rare. *Twin counter-rotating main rotors, no tail rotor, complicated double-finned tail assembly.*

Unless you are near a Russian naval fleet on maneuvers, this is the only twin-rotor helicopter you will ever see. The Soviet naval helicopters have both of their counter-rotating main rotors mounted on a single mast, and have tails resembling the Huskie. Huskies were once seen at every U.S. Air Force base, where they were used as firefighting and rescue craft. The Huskie was a common sight in Vietnam; now in civilian use only, and extremely rare.

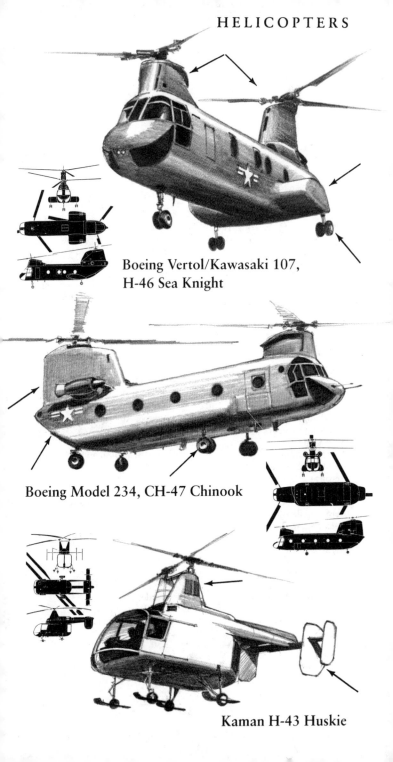

HELICOPTERS

Boeing Vertol/Kawasaki 107,
H-46 Sea Knight

Boeing Model 234, CH-47 Chinook

Kaman H-43 Huskie

Index

AT-8, Cessna Bobcat, 136
AT-19, Stinson Reliant, 56
AV-8B, McDonnell Douglas Harrier, 180
Avanti, Piaggio P180, 146
Avenger, Grumman TBF-1, 48
Aviat Christen Eagle, 10
Aviat Christen Husky A-1, 70
Aviat Pitts S-1, S-2, 10
Aviocar, CASA, 118
Avtek 400A, 146
Ayres Thrush, Bull Thrush, Turbo Thrush, 20
Aztec, Piper PA23, 94

B-1, Rockwell, 190
B-2, Northrop Stealth Bomber, 192
B-25, Mitchell, 138
B-26, Douglas, 138
B-52, Boeing Stratofortress, 190
Baby Lakes, 10
BAC 111, 158
BAe T-45 Goshawk, 178
Bandeirante, Embraer, 126
Baron, Beech D55, 58, 98
Beaver, de Havilland DHC2, 52
Beech 17 Staggerwing, 2
Beech 18, (C-45), 134
Beech 50 Twin Bonanza, 98
Beech 76 Duchess, 92
Beech 95 Travel Air, 98
Beech 99 Airliner, 126
Beech 1900, 1900D, 128
Beech B60 Duke, 100
Beech Baron D55, 58, 98
Beech Bonanza 35, F33A, 34
Beech Bonanza A36, 34
Beech King Air, 110
Beech Mentor, T-34A, 46
Beech Musketeer, 28
Beech Queen Air, 110
Beech Sierra, 28
Beech Skipper, 26
Beech Sport, 28
Beech Starship I, 146
Beech Sundowner, 28
Beech Super King Air (T-44, U-12, C-12), 110
Beech T-34C Mentor, 170
Beech U-21 Seminole, 110
Beech U-8, 110
Beechjet 400A, Mitsubishi Diamond, 154

Bell 206 JetRanger, LongRanger (OH-58 Kiowa), 206
Bell 212, 412, 208
Bell 214 ST, 208
Bell 222, 206
Bell AH-1 HueyCobra, Seacobra, Super Cobra, 210
Bell Model 47, 194
Bell OH-58D Kiowa, SeaRanger, 210
Bellanca Citabria, 60
Bellanca Cruiseair, 44
Bellanca Cruisemaster, 44
Bellanca Decathlon, 60
Bellanca Scout, 60
Bird Dog, Cessna O-1, 60
Blackhawk, Sikorsky, 214
Bobcat, Cessna (AT-8, C-78), 136
Boeing 707, 720, 166
Boeing 727, 160
Boeing 737-200, -300, -400, -500, 162
Boeing 747-200, -300, -400, 747SP, 168
Boeing 757, 162
Boeing 767-200, -300, 164
Boeing 777, 164
Boeing B-52 Stratofortress, 190
Boeing Model 234, CH-47 Chinook, 218
Boeing Vertol/Kawasaki 107, CH-46 Sea Knight, 218
Boeing/Stearman Kaydet, 4
Bonanza 35, F33A, 34
Borate Bomber, Grumman, 48
Brantly-Hynes 305, 198
Brantly-Hynes B-2, 198
Brasilia, Embraer, 126
Brave, 18
British Aerospace 125 (C-29), 154
British Aerospace 748, 130
British Aerospace BAe146-100, -200, -300, 166
British Aerospace Jetstream 31, 128
Britten-Norman Islander, 116
Britten-Norman Trislander MKIII, 116
Bronco, Rockwell OV-10, 170
BT-13, BT-15, SNV-1, Consolidated Vultee Valiant, 22
Buccaneer, Lake, 84
Buckeye, Rockwell T-2, 176

Business Jets (pp. 148–157)

Jet Airliners (pp. 158–169)

Military Aircraft (pp. 170–193)

Prop (pp. 170–175)

Small Jets (pp. 176–185)

Large Jets (pp. 186–193)

Helicopters (pp. 194–219)